THE
SLOWCOOKER LIBRARY

The Classic Casseroles for your Slow Cooker

THE SLOWCOOKER LIBRARY

The Classic Casseroles for your Slow Cooker

Catherine Atkinson

foulsham

LONDON • NEW YORK • TORONTO • SYDNEY

foulsham

The Oriel, Thames Valley Court, 183–187 Bath Road, Slough, Berkshire SL1 4AA, England

Foulsham books can be found in all good bookshops and direct from www.foulsham.com

ISBN: 978-0-572-03541-9

Printed in Great Britain by Martins the Printers Ltd, Berwick upon Tweed

contents

introduction

Casseroles can be wonderfully varied, ranging from rich winter stews to satisfy robust appetites to more delicate mixtures that are ideal for lunches and light suppers. Because casseroles need minimal attention, they are perfect for simple family meals and also ideal for relaxed entertaining.

Casseroles, stews, carbonnades, hot-pots and navarins are all names for what is essentially the same type of dish – meat and/or vegetables cooked in liquid in a cooking pot. Braises have a little less liquid and cook by a combination of simmering and steaming. Ragùs are especially rich casseroles. Originally, the word stew described dishes cooked on the stovetop, while casserole described dishes cooked in the oven, but now the names are largely interchangeable.

Slow cooking is the perfect way to create flavour-packed meals with the minimum effort and fuss. The basic principle is that food is cooked slowly at a low constant temperature. This has many advantages. One of the greatest is that it develops and enhances the flavour of food, while retaining its texture. It brings out the sweetness of vegetables and makes even the toughest meat meltingly tender; in fact, the less expensive cuts are better suited to slow cooking. Slow cookers are also environmentally friendly; their low wattage consumes about the same amount of electricity as a light bulb. A bonus is that food is unlikely to burn or over-dry. If you're out for the day, an extra hour of cooking won't ruin your recipe, so there's no need to worry if you get home a little later than planned. Timing is rarely critical, so if you are not ready when the casserole is, it can be left on the Low setting to keep it warm. The principles of slow cooking are incredibly simple, but do have a look at the following few pages before you begin.

choosing a slow cooker

Slow cookers now come in a huge range of colours, shapes, sizes and prices and these factors need to be considered before you make your choice.

Appearance is the first thing you'll notice. You'll find contemporary stainless steel, vibrant coloured and pristine white models as well as the rustic-looking cream and brown versions. The heat-resistant lid may be ceramic or toughened glass. The advantage of the latter is that you can monitor the food's progress without having to lift the lid and lose precious heat. Originally only round cookers were available; these are excellent for casserole making but the more modern oval version is a better buy if you entertain often as it's perfect for pot-roasting larger cuts of meat or want to casserole whole fish fillets.

The size of slow cookers ranges from a tiny 600 ml/1 pint/ 2½ cup cooking pot to a massive 6.5 litre/11¼ pint/27¼ cup, so choose a size that suits your needs. These recipes mainly serve four, so a 4 litre/7 pint/16 cup in size is about right.

using and caring for your slow cooker

Because slow cooker models vary, make sure you read the manufacturer's instructions before using yours for the first time. Some slow cookers need to be preheated before you start cooking; others advise against heating the slow cooker when empty. You should also check to see whether yours is dishwasherproof and whether it can be used under the grill (broiler) and in the oven, in the microwave or the freezer.

Before using for the first time, wash the ceramic cooking pot in hot soapy water, rinse well and dry. You may notice a slight odour as the slow cooker heats up; this is caused by the burning off of manufacturing residues and should disappear after the first few uses. Don't worry if the ceramic glaze becomes slightly crazed; this is perfectly normal.

You'll notice that the recipes advise using hot, not boiling, water and stock when adding it straight to the cooking pot. Never pour boiling water into the cold cooking pot (you can do so when it is already warm or hot) or plunge it into cold water immediately after use as this could crack it. Remember that it is an electrical appliance, so the outer casing should be wiped clean and never immersed in or filled with water.

When following a recipe, bear in mind that every model is slightly different and, even when using the same settings, some will cook much faster than others. For this reason a range of cooking times is given; you may need to use the shorter or the longer time or somewhere between the two. After trying a few recipes, you will know whether your slow cooker is faster or slower and you will be able to adjust the recipe cooking times accordingly.

During cooking, steam condenses on the lid of the slow cooker, then trickles back into the pot, helping to retain heat and reduce strong cooking smells. Unless a recipe tells you to stir a dish part-way through cooking, it should be left undisturbed and you should avoid lifting the lid.

using and caring for your slow cooker

slow cooker safety

The slow cooker is an extremely safe appliance, but common-sense precautions should be followed. Although it cooks at a low temperature, the outer casing, lid and the food inside the slow cooker may get extremely hot, so you should always use oven gloves when removing the ceramic cooking pot. Stand the slow cooker on a heat-resistant surface when in use, away from the edge where it might accidentally get knocked off, and make sure that the mains lead is tucked safely behind it. Take extra care that it's out of reach if you have young children or inquisitive pets living or staying with you.

Slow cookers cook food at a relatively low heat – around 90°C/195°F on the Low setting to about 150°C/300°F on the High setting. Any bacteria present in food is destroyed at 74°C/165°F, so as long as it's cooked for the correct time the temperature of the slow cooker will ensure that the food is safe to eat. You should take care, however, not to reduce the cooking temperature:

- Do not lift the lid during the cooking time unless the recipe specifies this.

- Ideally ingredients should be at room temperature when you start to cook. If you are using large amounts of frozen vegetables, it's a good idea to set the slow cooker on High or Auto for the first hour of cooking. Never add frozen or part-frozen meat to the slow cooker.

- You may need to increase the cooking time slightly when the kitchen temperature is extremely cold.

- Avoid placing the slow cooker in a draughty place or near an open window.

Always check that meat is thoroughly cooked, particularly poultry and pork. A meat thermometer is a good investment if you cook portions or larger cuts of meat as it will ensure they are sufficiently cooked without drying out and losing moistness. The meat is ready when the pointer on the dial reaches the appropriate wording; there are indications for types of meat including chicken, beef, lamb and pork, as well as readings within some of those categories for rare, medium and well-cooked meat.

cooking times

The cooking temperatures and settings vary on different models, but most have four settings: Off, Low, High and Auto. Some models have an additional Medium setting. At the lowest temperature the food will barely simmer; at the highest it will boil very gently. When set to Auto, the cooking temperature will build up to High, then remain at this temperature for an hour or so before automatically switching to Low. This setting is desirable if you are using frozen vegetables in your cooking without defrosting them first. Foods such as cuts of poultry, like chicken quarters and whole thighs (but not breasts or chopped chicken) should always be cooked on High or Auto for at least the first hour. Food should be monitored when using the High setting as some liquid will evaporate. Some flexibility can be introduced to the total cooking time by adjusting the temperature settings; for dishes such as soups, braises and casseroles, the cooking can be shortened or extended to suit your needs by changing the temperature setting. As a rough guide, the cooking time on Low is about double that of High.

Low	Auto or Medium	High
2–4	$1\frac{1}{2}$–$2\frac{1}{2}$	1–2
6–8	4–6	3–4
8–10	6–8	5–6

If at the end of the cooking time the food is not quite ready, replace the lid and switch the slow cooker to High to speed up the cooking process. Once ready, many dishes, especially casseroles and soups, can be kept hot for an hour or more without any risk of spoiling, by switching the slow cooker to Low.

If you are planning to go out for the day and your chosen recipe does not take as many hours to cook as you will be away, you can use a time-delay plug so that the start of cooking is delayed by several hours. This is particularly useful if you are including a large amount of frozen vegetables, which will then have a chance to thaw during this time and come up to room temperature before cooking starts. If you are going to delay the start of cooking, it's important that all the ingredients – including stock – are cold (preferably chilled) when added to the ceramic cooking pot. Never use a time-delay plug when cooking chicken or when the kitchen will be warm; e.g. on a sunny day or if the central heating will be on before cooking commences.

Modern slow cookers tend to cook at a slightly higher temperature than those that are ten or more years old, so if you have a newer model, check whether the food is ready at the minimum suggested cooking time when following the first few recipes.

making casseroles

There are two basic ways of making slow cooker casseroles; a simple one-step method, where cold raw ingredients are placed in the ceramic cooking pot and a second method in which the meat and some or all of the vegetables are fried beforehand.

making a one-step casserole

Here all the ingredients are placed in the ceramic cooking pot without pre-frying – a simple Irish stew (see page 74) being a classic example. This reduces preparation time and is also suitable for those on a reduced-fat diet. For the tenderest results, casseroles should be cooked on a Low setting and this is also ideal if you plan to be out all day.

making a pre-fried casserole

This method is used for the majority of casseroles, because it adds colour and an intense rich flavour. The natural sugars in the ingredients are broken down by pre-frying and the sweet, complex flavours are released. While pre-cooking meat improves the taste and appearance of the cooked casserole, it is also useful to give vegetables the same treatment, especially onions, because they take much longer to tenderise than meat in a slow cooker.

adapting your own recipes

Many conventional recipes can be adapted for cooking in a slow cooker. The easiest way to adapt a recipe is to find a similar one in this book and use it as a guide. Remember that there is less evaporation in the slow cooker than in conventional cooking, so reduce the liquid content by about a third. Check towards the end of cooking time and add more boiling liquid if necessary.

slow cooking hints and tips

- During cooking, steam condenses on the lid of the slow cooker, then trickles back into the pot, helping to retain heat and reduce strong cooking smells. Make sure that the lid is placed centrally on the cooking pot. Unless a recipe tells you to stir a dish part-way through cooking, it should be left undisturbed and you should avoid lifting the lid. If you do need to lift the lid during cooking other than when specified in a recipe (to add a forgotten ingredient, for example), add an extra 10–15 minutes cooking time to make up for the heat loss.
- Allow a 5 cm/2 in distance between the food and top of the ceramic cooking pot. While all of the recipes here follow this, bear this in mind if you decide to double the ingredients in a recipe to make a larger amount.
- Alcohol evaporates more slowly in the slow cooker than other liquids, so don't increase the amount given in the recipe or its flavour may be overpowering.
- Onions and root vegetables, such as carrots, take longer to cook than meat as the liquid simmers rather than boils. These should be cut into smallish, even-sized chunks before adding to the cooking pot. If possible, place them at the bottom of the cooking pot, which is the hottest part.
- Vegetables with a high water content such as pumpkins and courgettes (zucchini) will cook quickly, so add them towards the end of cooking time or place towards the top of the cooking pot, rather than nearer the base.
- It is preferable for frozen vegetables to be thawed before adding but it isn't essential. If time allows, defrost them in the

refrigerator for several hours or overnight or spread them out on kitchen paper (paper towels) at room temperature. If adding frozen vegetables, the dish will take a little longer to cook than if defrosted ones are used.

- Ordinary long-grain rice doesn't cook well in the slow cooker, but easy-cook (converted) rice, also known as 'parboiled', will cook to perfection. It has been steamed under pressure, ensuring the grains remain separate and making it difficult to overcook. Easy-cook brown and easy-cook basmati rice are also available.
- Fresh herbs added at the beginning of long cooking will lose their colour and pungency. Use dried herbs at the start of cooking and add fresh ones towards the end.
- Many recipes contain alternative cooking times within the method which may be more convenient if you have a lot of time available.

slow cooking hints and tips

notes on the recipes

- Do not mix metric, imperial and American measures. Follow one set only.
- All spoon measurements are level: 1 tsp = 5 ml; 1 tbsp = 15 ml
- American terms are given in brackets.
- The ingredients are listed in the order in which they are used in the recipe.
- Eggs are medium unless otherwise stated. If you use a different size, adjust the amount of liquid added to obtain the right consistency.
- Always wash, peel, core, deseed, etc. fresh foods before use. If vegetables or fruits are to be used unpeeled it states this in the recipe. Ensure that all produce is as fresh as possible and in good condition.
- Generally use medium-sized vegetables, unless the recipe indicates otherwise.
- The use of strongly flavoured items such as garlic and chilli depends on personal taste, so adjust accordingly.
- All cooking times are approximate and are intended as a guide only. Get to know your slow cooker; you will soon know if it cooks a little faster or slower than the times given here.
- Can and packet sizes depend on the particular brand.
- Vegetarian recipes are marked with a symbol. Those who eat fish but not meat will find plenty of additional recipes containing seafood to enjoy. Omit dairy products or substitute with a vegetarian alternative if you prefer. Recipes may use processed foods, so vegetarians should check the specific product labels to be certain of their suitability.

V
Suitable for Vegetarians

beef

The slow cooker is renowned for producing **wonderful** meat casseroles, stews and **braises**. With beef, it truly excels, making even the toughest cuts **meltingly** tender and both developing and **enhancing** their flavour.

In this chapter you'll find a variety of recipes to suit every taste and budget. There are classic winter warmers such as Boeuf Bourguignon (see page 22) and Beef Carbonnade (see page 34), 24 whole cuts such as Orange and Mustard-glazed Silverside (see page 28) and other cuts including oxtail. Veal comes from young calves so is tender and lean and therefore not well suited to cooking in the slow cooker. Exceptions are shoulder of veal, which is often cut into chunks for casseroles (and labelled 'casserole veal' and the knuckle, which can be cut into slices and used to make the Italian casserole Osso Bucco (see page 64).

When it comes to choosing beef for casserole cooking, don't go for the most expensive cuts believing that they will produce a better casserole. Ideal beef cuts for slow cooker casseroles are generally the cheaper ones such as brisket and chuck steak as they have a looser texture. During cooking the fibres open up and allow moisture to penetrate, creating a rich, tasty gravy. More expensive cuts, such as fine-grained and densely textured sirloin (porterhouse) steak, are less suitable for slow cooking because the tightness of the fibres prevents them absorbing the liquid around them. This means that although they become tender when cooked in a slow cooker, the casserole will lack succulence and flavour.

Beef should be kept covered on a low shelf in the refrigerator. Pre-packed meat can be left in its packaging and used by the date given on the packet. When buying loose meat and steaks, use within 2–3 days; larger cuts should keep for up to 4 days; your butcher will advise you.

boeuf bourguignon

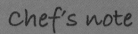

4 | **20** MINS | **3-4** hrs HIGH | creamy mashed potatoes and a green vegetable

Chef's note

This robust and much-loved classic comes from the Burgundy region of France. The beef is slowly cooked in a rich, red wine sauce with button onions, mushrooms and smoked streaky bacon. Use a full-bodied wine for the best flavour.

175 g/6 oz **button (pearl) onions**, unpeeled

30 ml/2 tbsp **olive oil**

100 g/4 oz rindless **smoked streaky bacon**, cut into small pieces

100 g/4 oz **baby button mushrooms**

2 **garlic cloves**, crushed or 10 ml/2 tsp garlic purée (paste)

250 ml/8 fl oz/1 cup **beef stock**

700 g/1½ lb lean **braising or chuck steak**, trimmed and cut into 5 cm/2 in cubes

10 ml/2 tsp **plain (all-purpose) flour**

250 ml/8 fl oz/1 cup **red wine**

1 sprig of fresh **thyme** or 2.5 ml/½ tsp dried thyme

1 **bay leaf**

Salt and freshly ground black pepper

30 ml/2 tbsp chopped **fresh parsley**

1 Put the onions in a heatproof bowl and pour over enough boiling water to cover. Leave for 5 minutes.

2 Meanwhile, heat 15 ml/1 tbsp of the oil in a frying pan, add the bacon and fry until lightly browned. Transfer to the ceramic cooking pot using a slotted spoon, leaving all the fat and juices behind.

3 Drain the onions and peel off the skins when cool enough to handle. Add to the frying pan and cook gently until they begin to brown. Add the mushrooms and garlic and cook for 2 minutes, stirring. Transfer the vegetables to the cooking pot. Pour the stock over, cover with the lid and switch on the slow cooker to High or Low.

4 Heat the remaining oil in the frying pan and fry the beef cubes until a rich, dark-brown colour on all sides. Sprinkle the flour over the meat and stir well. Gradually pour in the wine, stirring all the time, until the sauce is bubbling and thickened. Add to the cooking pot with the thyme, bay leaf, salt and pepper.

5 Cook the casserole for 3–4 hours on High or 6–8 hours on Low, or until the meat and vegetables are very tender. Remove the thyme sprig and bay leaf.

6 Sprinkle with the parsley and serve with creamy mashed potatoes and a green vegetable such as French (green) beans.

beef carbonnade

4

20 MINS

3-4 hrs AUTO

crusty French bread

Chef's note

You need only a small amount of beer to enrich this well-known Belgian dish, so it's a good idea to choose one that you enjoy drinking as well. Serve with creamy mashed potatoes or simply with plenty of warmed crusty bread to soak up the delicious sauce. You can use red or white wine vinegar.

700 g/1½ lb lean **braising or chuck steak**, trimmed

30 ml/2 tbsp **sunflower oil**

1 large **onion**, thinly sliced

2 **garlic cloves**, crushed or 10 ml/2 tsp garlic purée (paste)

10 ml/2 tsp **soft brown sugar**

15 ml/1 tbsp **plain (all-purpose) flour**

250 ml/8 fl oz/1 cup **light ale**

250 ml/8 fl oz/1 cup **beef stock**

5 ml/1 tsp **wine vinegar**

1 **bay leaf**

Salt and freshly ground black pepper

Chopped **fresh parsley**, to garnish (optional)

1   Cut the meat into pieces about 5 cm/2 in square and 1 cm/½ in thick. Heat 15 ml/1 tbsp of the oil in a frying pan and brown the meat on all sides. Transfer to the ceramic cooking pot with a slotted spoon, leaving the juices behind in the pan.

2   Add the remaining oil to the pan. Add the onion and cook gently for 5 minutes. Stir in the garlic and sugar, then sprinkle the flour over, stirring to mix. Gradually add the ale and bring to the boil. Let it bubble for a minute, then turn off the heat.

3   Pour the mixture over the beef, then stir in the stock and vinegar. Add the bay leaf and season with salt and pepper. Cover with the lid. There are two ways to cook this carbonnade. Switch on to Auto and cook for 3–4 hours or switch on to High, cook for 1 hour then reduce the heat to Low and cook for a further 5–7 hours or until the beef is very tender.

4   Remove the bay leaf and adjust the seasoning if necessary.

5   Serve the casserole straight away, garnished with a little chopped fresh parsley if liked and accompanied with crusty French bread.

Tip

• For a crunchy garlic topping, arrange 12 thin slices of French bread, lightly toasted and spread with 50 g/2 oz/¼ cup butter blended with 2 crushed garlic cloves and some salt and pepper on top of the casserole or transfer to a heatproof casserole dish (Dutch oven). Grill (broil) until golden brown and crisp.

spiced beef with horseradish

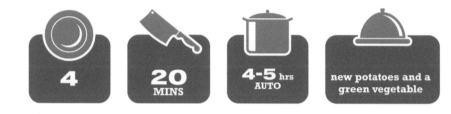

4 | 20 MINS | 4-5 hrs AUTO | new potatoes and a green vegetable

The warm spiciness of this casserole is achieved with a mixture of creamed horseradish, ginger and curry powder. It may sound an unusual combination but long slow cooking develops and mellows all the flavours.

1 **onion**, chopped

30 ml/2 tbsp **creamed horseradish sauce**

15 ml/1 tbsp **Worcestershire sauce**

450 ml/¾ pint/2 cups hot (not boiling) **beef stock**

15 ml/1 tbsp **plain (all-purpose) flour**

5 ml/1 tsp **medium curry powder**

2.5 ml/½ tsp **ground ginger**

5 ml/1 tsp **dark brown sugar**

700 g/1½ lb lean **braising or chuck steak**, cubed

Salt and freshly ground black pepper

30 ml/2 tbsp chopped **fresh or frozen parsley**

1   Put the onion in the ceramic cooking pot. Stir the horseradish and Worcestershire sauce into the stock and pour over the onion.

2   Switch on the slow cooker to Auto or Low and leave for 3–4 minutes while preparing and measuring the remaining ingredients.

3   Mix the flour, curry powder, ginger and sugar together in a bowl. Add the beef and toss to coat the cubes evenly in the spice mixture. Add to the cooking pot and season with salt and pepper.

4   Cover the ceramic cooking pot with the lid and cook for 4–5 hours on Auto or 6–7 hours on Low or until the beef is really tender.

5   Stir in the parsley and adjust the seasoning if necessary.

6   Serve with new potatoes and a green vegetable such as steamed shredded cabbage.

Tip
• Use ginger purée (paste) and curry paste instead of the ground ginger and curry powder, if you prefer.

orange & mustard glazed silverside

4-6

20 MINS plus soaking time

4 hrs AUTO

selection of roasted vegetables

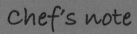

Chef's note

Although silverside is surrounded by a thin layer of fat, it is a very lean cut of beef and tends to be dry if simply oven-roasted. Here it is slowly pot-roasted until beautifully tender and moist, then glazed and finished in the oven.

1.6 kg/3½ lb piece of boned, **salted silverside (top round)**

1 small **orange**

1 **onion**, cut into wedges

2 **carrots**, sliced

1 **celery stick**, chopped

8 **whole cloves**

75 g/3 oz/⅓ cup **soft brown sugar**

5 ml/1 tsp **mustard powder**

5 ml/1 tsp **ground cinnamon**

1 Soak the meat in cold water and cover for several hours or overnight in the refrigerator to remove excess saltiness.

2 Rinse the silverside and put in the ceramic cooking pot. Thinly pare the zest from the orange and add to the pot with the onion, carrots and celery. Set aside the orange for use later.

3 Pour over just enough cold water to cover the meat. Switch on the slow cooker to High or Auto. After 1 hour (or when the water is gently bubbling), skim off any scum, re-cover with the lid and leave on Auto or reduce the temperature to Low.

4 Cook for a further 3 hours or until the meat is tender. Leave the silverside to cool in the liquid for 1 hour.

5 Preheat the oven to 180°C/350°F/gas 4/fan oven 160°C. Remove the silverside from the liquid and pat dry with kitchen paper (paper towels). Put in a roasting tin and press the cloves into the fat, spacing evenly all over the meat.

6 Cut the orange in half and squeeze out the juice. Put the brown sugar, mustard powder and cinnamon in a bowl. Stir in enough orange juice to make a thick paste. Spread over the meat.

7 Roast in the oven for 45 minutes, basting once or twice during cooking, or until well-browned.

8 Serve hot with a selection of roasted vegetables. Alternatively, leave the beef to cool and serve cold.

Tip
• If serving cold, you can press the meat to give it a denser texture and make it easier to slice. Place it in a tightly-fitting dish or foil-lined tin. Spoon a few tablespoonfuls of the cooking liquid over, then cover with a board or plate and put a heavy weight on top. Refrigerate for several hours.

boeuf en daube

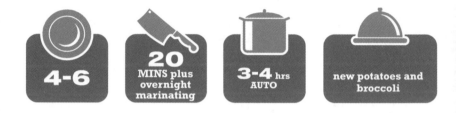

4-6

20 MINS plus overnight marinating

3-4 hrs AUTO

new potatoes and broccoli

Chef's note

A daube is a cross between a pot roast and a casserole, in which a whole piece of meat is cooked in a flavoursome liquid, in this case, wine and tomatoes. Instead of thickening with flour or by reduction, the sauce is a purée of the delicious gravy and vegetables.

1.25 kg/2½ lb piece of **topside or top rump beef**

2 **bay leaves**

2 **allspice berries**

450 ml/¾ pint/2 cups **red wine**

30 ml/2 tbsp **olive oil**

50 g/2 oz **smoked bacon lardons**

1 **onion**, chopped

2 **carrots**, chopped

1 **celery stick**, chopped

30 ml/2 tbsp **sun-dried tomato purée (paste)**

400 ml/14 fl oz/1¾ cups **beef stock**

Salt and freshly ground black pepper

1   Place the meat in a deep bowl slightly bigger than the joint with the bay leaves and allspice. Pour in the wine, turn the meat, then cover the bowl and leave to marinate in the refrigerator overnight.

2   Take out the meat and pat it dry on kitchen paper (paper towels) and reserve the wine. Heat the oil in a large heavy frying pan and brown the meat on all sides. Transfer it to a plate and set aside.

3   Add the bacon lardons and chopped onion to the pan and fry for 5 minutes until just beginning to brown, then add the carrots and celery and cook for a further 2–3 minutes. Arrange a single layer of bacon and vegetables on the base of the ceramic cooking pot, then place the meat on top, adding any juices that have accumulated on the plate.

4   Tuck the remaining bacon and vegetables around the sides of the meat. Add the wine to the frying pan with the tomato purée and heat for a minute or two until warm but not boiling. Add to the ceramic cooking pot. Pour in enough stock to just cover the meat and vegetables, then season well with salt and pepper.

5   Cover with the lid and cook on Auto for 3–4 hours or on Low for 4–6 hours, until the meat is very tender.

6   Using a slotted spoon, lift the meat out of the ceramic cooking pot and keep warm. Discard the bay leaves and allspice berries, then pour the vegetables and sauce into a food processor and blend until smooth.

7   Taste and adjust the seasoning if necessary, then reheat the sauce until boiling in a saucepan.

8   Carve the meat into thin slices and serve with the sauce, new potatoes and broccoli or another green vegetable.

crumble-topped beef casserole

4   **25** MINS   **3-5** hrs LOW plus 25 mins in the oven   a green vegetable

Chef's note

Cooking in the slow cooker doesn't mean you can't enjoy meals with crunchy toppings such as this crumble. It does take a little more effort as it's finished in the oven but both the basic casserole and crumble topping are incredibly easy to prepare.

700 g/1½ lb lean **braising or chuck steak**, cubed

450 g/1 lb **frozen 'root roasting' vegetables**, thawed if possible

1 x 400 g/14 oz/large **can of chopped tomatoes**

2.5 ml/½ tsp **dried mixed herbs**

250 ml/8 fl oz/1 cup boiling **beef stock**

Salt and freshly ground black pepper

For the crumble topping:

100 g/4 oz/1 cup **plain (all-purpose) flour**

1.5 ml/¼ tsp **English mustard powder** (optional)

50 g/2 oz/¼ cup chilled **butter**, cut into small cubes

50 g/2 oz/½ cup **grated Cheddar cheese**

1   Put the beef and vegetables in the ceramic cooking pot. Add the tomatoes, herbs and stock and season with salt and pepper.

2   Stir, then cover with the lid and cook on Low for 3–5 hours or until the beef and vegetables are very tender.

3   Meanwhile make the topping. Put the flour, mustard powder and butter in a food processor and whiz together until the mixture resembles fine breadcrumbs (or rub in with your fingertips in a bowl). Add the cheese and season with salt and pepper and briefly process again to mix.

4   Just before the end of the casserole's cooking time, preheat the oven to 190°C/375°F/gas 5/fan oven 170°C. If your ceramic cooking pot isn't ovenproof, transfer the casserole to an ovenproof dish (Dutch oven). Sprinkle the crumble topping over the casserole.

5   Bake uncovered for 20–25 minutes until golden brown.

6   Serve straight away with a green vegetable such as peas.

Tip

• Bags of frozen 'root-roasting' vegetables usually contain a mixture of onions, carrots, parsnips and swede (rutabaga), all cut into small chunks.

pot-roasted brisket in beer

4-6

20 MINS plus marinating time

4-6 hrs AUTO

complete meal in itself

1.25 kg/2½ lb rolled **brisket**

300 ml/½ pint/1¼ cups **pale ale**

Salt and freshly ground black pepper

25 g/1 oz/2 tbsp **beef dripping**, **white vegetable fat** or **sunflower oil**

2 **onions**, cut into 8 wedges

2 **carrots**, quartered

2 **celery sticks**, thickly sliced

2 sprigs of **fresh thyme**

2 **bay leaves**

2 **whole cloves**

150 ml/¼ pint/⅔ cup boiling **beef stock**

15 ml/1 tbsp **cornflour (cornstarch)**

1   Place the meat in a bowl just large enough to hold it and pour the pale ale over. Cover and leave to marinate in the refrigerator for at least 8 hours, or overnight if preferred, turning several times if possible.

2   Drain the meat, reserving the ale and wipe dry. Season well with salt and pepper. Heat the dripping, vegetable fat or oil in a large, heavy pan until hot. Add the meat and turn frequently until well browned all over. Lift the meat on to a plate.

3   Pour away some of the fat in the pan, then add the onions, carrots and celery. Cook for a few minutes until lightly browned and beginning to soften. Arrange a single layer of vegetables in the base of the ceramic cooking pot. Put the beef on top, then add the remaining vegetables around the sides of the meat. Tuck in the thyme, bay leaves and cloves.

4   Pour the beer marinade over the beef, followed by the beef stock. Cover with the lid and cook for 4–6 hours on Auto or 5–8 hours on Low, or until the meat and vegetables are cooked through and tender. Turn the meat and baste with the gravy once or twice during cooking.

5   Lift out the meat and place on a warmed serving plate or board. Cover with foil and leave to rest for 10 minutes before carving into thick slices.

6   Meanwhile, skim any fat from the juices and gravy in the ceramic cooking pot. Blend the cornflour with a little cold water in a saucepan, then strain in the stock (keeping the vegetables, discarding the bay leaves and thyme). Bring to the boil, whisking until bubbling and thickened. Taste and adjust the seasoning if necessary.

7   Serve the rich gravy with the beef and vegetables.

goulash with dumplings

Chef's note

This classic Hungarian dish, richly seasoned with sweet paprika, is topped with little dumplings made from breadcrumbs and flavoured with herbs and caraway seeds.

1 **onion**, finely chopped

1 **garlic clove**, crushed or 5 ml/ 1 tsp garlic purée (paste)

300 ml/½ pint/1¼ cups very hot (not boiling) **beef stock**

700 g/1½ lb lean **chuck or braising steak**, cubed

10 ml/2 tsp **paprika**

175 g/6 oz **white cabbage**

200 g/7 oz **whole baby carrots**

1 x 400 g/14 oz/large **can of chopped tomatoes with herbs**

Salt and freshly ground black pepper

For the dumplings:

1 **egg**

15 ml/1 tbsp **milk**

15 ml/1 tbsp chopped **fresh or frozen parsley**

1.5 ml/¼ tsp **caraway seeds**

75 g/3 oz/1½ cups **fresh white breadcrumbs**

1   Put the onion and garlic in the ceramic cooking pot. Pour in the stock, cover with the lid and switch the slow cooker on to Low. Leave for a few minutes while preparing the remaining ingredients.

2   Sprinkle the cubed beef with the paprika. Finely shred the cabbage. Add the beef and cabbage to the slow cooker with the carrots and tomatoes. Season with salt and pepper, then cover and cook for 3–5 hours or until the beef is very tender.

3   Turn up the slow cooker to High and allow 30 minutes for it to come up to temperature.

4   Meanwhile, beat the egg and milk together in a bowl. Stir in the parsley and caraway seeds and a little salt and pepper. Add the breadcrumbs and mix well. With wet hands, shape the dumpling mixture into 12 walnut-sized balls.

5   Quickly add the dumplings to the slow cooker, placing them carefully on top of the casserole. Re-cover and cook for a further 30 minutes.

6   Serve at once, topped with a little soured cream or crème fraîche.

chilli beef & tomato casserole

4	20 MINS	2-3 hrs AUTO	garden peas or petits pois

Chef's note

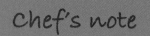

This colourful, all-in-one beef and rice supper dish is simmered in a rich tomato sauce with the spicy addition of chilli. As a bonus, none of the ingredients need pre-cooking, which speeds up the preparation time.

225 g/8 oz lean **minced (ground) beef**

1 **onion**, finely chopped

250 ml/8 fl oz/1 cup **passata (sieved tomatoes)**

120 ml/4 fl oz/⅓ cup boiling **beef or vegetable stock**

2.5 ml/½ tsp dried **chilli flakes** or 5 ml/1 tsp chilli powder

2.5 ml/½ tsp **dried mixed herbs**

Salt and freshly ground black pepper

175 g/6 oz/¾ cup **easy-cook (converted) rice**

1 x 200 g/7 oz/small **can of sweetcorn**, drained

1 **red or yellow (bell) pepper**, seeded and chopped

1   Crumble about half of the minced beef evenly over the bottom of the ceramic cooking pot. Top with about half of the chopped onion, then sprinkle over the remaining beef followed by the rest of the onion.

2   In a large jug, stir together the passata, stock, chilli flakes or powder, mixed herbs, salt and pepper. Pour half over the beef and onion layers.

3   Sprinkle the rice evenly over the top, followed by the sweetcorn and chopped pepper. Pour over the remaining tomato mixture.

4   Cover with the lid and cook for 2–3 hours on Auto or 4–5 hours on Low, or until the rice and beef are tender and most of the juices have been absorbed.

5   Serve straight away with garden peas or petits pois, if liked.

Tip

• It's important to crumble the minced beef between your fingers as you add it to the cooking pot to prevent it from sticking together in large clumps as it cooks. Minced pork or turkey could also be used in this dish.

beef casserole with port

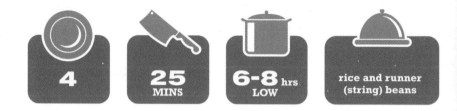

4

25 MINS

6-8 hrs LOW

rice and runner (string) beans

Chef's note

This is a rich and delicious dish with just a hint of sweetness from the treacle, giving it almost a Caribbean flavour.

175 g/6 oz **button (pearl) onions**, unpeeled

30 ml/2 tbsp **sunflower oil**

700 g/1½ lb lean **braising or chuck steak**, trimmed and cut into 5 cm/2 in cubes

150 g/5 oz **baby button mushrooms**

1 **garlic clove**, crushed or 5 ml/ 1 tsp garlic purée (paste)

15 ml/1 tbsp **plain (all-purpose) flour**

300 ml/½ pint/1¼ cups **beef stock**

2 **oranges**

15 ml/1 tbsp **tomato purée (paste)**

15 ml/1 tbsp **black treacle (molasses)**

30 ml/2 tbsp **port**

Salt and freshly ground black pepper

1   Put the onions in a heatproof bowl and pour over enough boiling water to cover. Leave for 5–10 minutes while browning the beef.

2   Heat the oil in a frying pan. Add the beef and cook for 5 minutes, turning the pieces frequently until browned all over. Transfer to the ceramic cooking pot with a slotted spoon, leaving any fat and juices behind.

3   Drain the onions and peel off the skins when cool enough to handle. Add to the frying pan with the mushrooms and cook gently until they begin to brown.

4   Stir in the garlic, then push the mixture to one side. Sprinkle the flour over the fat and juices in the pan. Stir well, then gradually add the stock and bring to the boil. Remove from the heat.

5   Remove the zest from the oranges using a zester. Cut the oranges in half and squeeze out the juice. Add the zest and juice to the pan. Stir in the tomato purée, black treacle and port. Season with salt and pepper. Pour the mixture over the beef in the ceramic cooking pot.

6   Cover with the lid and cook on Low for 6–8 hours or until the beef and onions are very tender.

7   Serve with rice and runner beans or another green vegetable.

Tip
- If you don't have a zester, either grate off the zest on the fine holes of a grater or pare the zest thinly from the oranges with a potato peeler then cut into fine julienne strips.

steak & kidney casserole

4 **25 MINS** **5-7 hrs LOW** creamed potatoes and carrots

chef's note

A small amount of lambs' kidney adds a subtle yet unique flavour to this dish. However, not everyone is keen on kidneys, in which case you can simply add a few extra mushrooms instead.

4 **lambs' kidneys**

15 ml/1 tbsp **plain (all-purpose) flour**

Salt and freshly ground black pepper

550 g/1¼ lb lean **braising or stewing steak**, trimmed and cut into 2 cm/½ in cubes

30 ml/2 tbsp **sunflower oil**

1 **onion**, chopped

175 g/6 oz **button mushrooms**, quartered

60 ml/4 tbsp **port**, **red wine** or extra stock

300 ml/½ pint/1¼ cups **beef stock**

10 ml/2 tsp **Worcestershire sauce** (optional)

2.5 ml/½ tsp **dried mixed herbs**

1   Halve the kidneys, remove the white core, then cut them into 1 cm/½ in chunks. Mix the flour with a little salt and pepper and use this mixture to coat the beef.

2   Heat 15 ml/1 tbsp of the oil in a frying pan, add the beef and fry over a moderately high heat in two batches until browned all over. Transfer to the ceramic cooking pot with a slotted spoon and switch on the slow cooker to Low. Brown the kidneys in the remaining fat in the pan and add them to the beef.

3   Heat the remaining oil in the frying pan, add the onion and cook for 5 minutes. Add the mushrooms and cook for 3–4 minutes until soft. Turn off the heat and stir in the port, red wine or extra stock.

4   Pour the onion and mushroom mixture over the meat and stir in the stock, Worcestershire sauce, if using, and herbs. Cover with the lid and cook for 5–7 hours or until the meat is very tender.

5   Serve straight away with creamed potatoes and carrots.

Variation

- To make a steak and kidney pie, spoon the meat and vegetables into a 1.5 litre/2½ pint/6 cup pie dish with a little of the sauce. Roll out 225 g/8 oz of puff pastry (paste) 5 cm/2 in larger than the dish. Cut a 2.5 cm/1 in strip from the edge and press on to the rim of the dish. Brush with beaten egg, then press the rolled-out pastry on top. Glaze with beaten egg, make a slit in the top, then bake on a baking (cookie) sheet at 200°C/400°F/gas 6/fan oven 180°C for 30 minutes until well risen and brown.

beef in guinness

| 4 | 30 MINS | 4-6 hrs LOW + 1 hr HIGH | a green vegetable |

chef's note

A really traditional recipe, cooking in beer gives a rich flavour and helps to tenderise the meat – and obviously Guinness adds that extra something.

30 ml/2 tbsp **sunflower oil**

700 g/1½ lb lean **braising or chuck steak**, trimmed and cut into 5 cm/2 in cubes

2 **onions**, thinly sliced

2 **carrots**, sliced

30 ml/2 tbsp **plain (all-purpose) flour**

300 ml/½ pint/1¼ cups **Guinness** or **stout**

10 ml/2 tsp **light brown sugar**

15 ml/1 tbsp **tomato purée (paste)**

15 ml/1 tbsp **Worcestershire sauce**

Salt and freshly ground black pepper

150 ml/¼ pint/⅔ cup boiling **beef stock**

1 **bay leaf**

For the dumplings:

100 g/4 oz/1 cup **self-raising flour**

5 ml/1 tsp **dry English mustard powder**

50 g/2 oz/½ cup **shredded (chopped) beef or vegetable suet**

30–45 ml/2–3 tbsp cold **water**

1   Heat the oil in a large heavy-based frying pan, add the beef and fry, turning frequently until browned all over. Transfer the meat to the ceramic cooking pot with a slotted spoon, leaving the fat and juices behind in the pan.

2   Add the onions to the frying pan and cook for 5 minutes or until beginning to brown. Add the carrots and cook for a further 2–3 minutes.

3   Sprinkle the flour over the vegetables and stir in. Gradually add the Guinness or stout, stirring all the time until thickened. Turn off the heat and stir in the sugar, tomato purée and Worcestershire sauce. Season with salt and pepper. Pour the mixture over the beef.

4   Add the beef stock and bay leaf to the ceramic cooking pot. Give the mixture a stir, then cover with the lid and cook on Low for 4–6 hours or until the beef is very tender.

5   Turn up the slow cooker to High and allow 30 minutes to come up to temperature. For the dumplings, sift the flour and mustard and 2.5 ml/½ tsp of salt into a bowl. Stir in the suet. Add enough water to make a soft dough. Shape into 16 balls and place on top of the casserole. Cook for a further 30 minutes, until the dumplings are well risen and light. Discard the bay leaf.

6   Serve straight away with a green vegetable, if liked.

Tip
• Add the dumplings quickly so that there isn't a drop in temperature and don't lift the lid while they are cooking or they may sink.

easy beef stroganoff

4 | **20** MINS | **5-7** hrs LOW | rice or buttered noodles

Chef's note

This famous Russian recipe is rumoured to have been created by Count Stroganoff's chef to use beef frozen by the Siberian climate. The only way it could be prepared was by cutting it into very fine strips. The dish is traditionally made with fillet steak, flash-fried in a pan. Here, braising steak – a less expensive alternative – is slow cooked until meltingly tender.

700 g/1½ lb good-quality **braising steak**, such as blade

30 ml/2 tbsp **plain (all-purpose) flour**

25 g/1 oz/2 tbsp **unsalted (sweet) butter**

30 ml/2 tbsp **olive oil**

1 **onion**, sliced

2 **garlic cloves**, crushed or 10 ml/2 tsp garlic purée (paste)

30 ml/2 tbsp **brandy**

5 ml/1 tsp **French mustard**

10 ml/2 tsp **tomato purée (paste)**

450 ml/¾ pint/2 cups hot **beef stock**

Salt and freshly ground black pepper

225 g/8 oz **chestnut** or **field mushrooms**, thinly sliced

1.5 ml/¼ tsp freshly grated **nutmeg**

150 ml/¼ pint/⅔ cup **crème fraîche** or **soured (dairy sour) cream**

30 ml/2 tbsp chopped **fresh or frozen parsley**

1. Cut the beef into thin strips about 5 mm/¼ in thick and 5 cm/ 2 in long. Lightly toss in the flour to coat. Heat half the butter and half the oil in a frying pan and quickly cook the beef until browned all over. Transfer to the ceramic cooking pot.

2. Add the remaining oil to the pan and cook the onion for 5 minutes, or until beginning to brown. Add the garlic and cook for a further minute, then turn off the heat and stir in the brandy, mustard and tomato purée. Add the mixture to the slow cooker.

3. Pour in the stock and season with salt and pepper. Gently stir the mixture, then cover the ceramic cooking pot with the lid and cook on Low for 5–7 hours (this includes the time to cook the mushroom mixture below).

4. Thirty minutes before the end of the cooking time, heat the remaining butter in a pan and gently cook the mushrooms until tender. Stir in the nutmeg, crème fraîche or soured cream and half the parsley. Bring the mixture to simmering point, then add to the casserole and stir well. Re-cover and cook for the remaining cooking time.

5. Serve the stroganoff sprinkled with the remaining parsley and accompanied by rice or buttered noodles.

Tip
- When slicing the beef into strips cut across the grain rather than with the grain, as this will make it more tender.

greek stifado

4 | **25** MINS | **5-7** hrs LOW | greek-style bread or pittas

This Mediterranean casserole contains new potatoes, artichokes, broad beans and olives. Ideal for easy entertaining, it is simple to make and smells and tastes absolutely wonderful.

12 **fresh or frozen baby onions**, thawed if possible

2 **garlic cloves**, crushed or 10 ml/2 tsp garlic purée (paste)

2.5 ml/½ tsp **ground cumin**

2.5 ml/½ tsp **ground cinnamon**

250 ml/8 fl oz/1 cup very hot (not boiling) **beef stock**

700 g/1½ lb lean **chuck or braising steak**, cubed

225 g/8 oz **baby new potatoes**

225 g/8 oz **fresh or frozen broad (fava) beans**, thawed if possible

50 g/2 oz/⅓ cup stoned (pitted) **Kalamata olives**, roughly chopped

1 x 400 g/14 oz/large **can of chopped tomatoes with herbs**

175 ml/6 fl oz/¾ cup **full-bodied red wine**

1 **bay leaf**

Freshly ground black pepper

1   If using fresh baby onions, put them in a heatproof bowl and pour over enough boiling water to cover. Leave until the water is tepid, then remove the onions and cut off the tops and root ends; the skins will slide off effortlessly.

2   Put the onions, garlic, cumin and cinnamon in the ceramic cooking pot and pour over the stock. Cover with the lid and switch on the slow cooker to Low. Leave for a few minutes while measuring and preparing the remaining ingredients.

3   Add the beef, potatoes, broad beans and olives to the cooking pot. Pour over the chopped tomatoes and wine, add the bay leaf and season with pepper.

4   Cover and cook for 5–7 hours on Low or until the onions and beef are tender. Discard the bay leaf.

5   Serve straight away on warmed plates or bowls with Greek-style bread or pittas.

Tip
- Also known as 'stifatho', this easy dish is sometimes made with rabbit rather than beef.

curried beef & pineapple

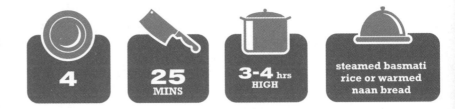

4 | **25** MINS | **3-4** hrs HIGH | steamed basmati rice or warmed naan bread

Chef's note

This mellow curry has just a hint of spicy flavour, so is ideal for those who don't enjoy really hot dishes. Cubes of lean lamb or pork can be used instead of beef, if preferred.

30 ml/2 tbsp **sunflower oil**

700 g/1½ lb lean **braising or chuck steak**, trimmed and cut into 5 cm/2 in cubes

2 **onions**, chopped

10 ml/2 tsp **mild curry powder** or curry paste

10 ml/2 tsp **wine vinegar**

30 ml/2 tbsp **apricot jam (conserve)**

1 x 200 g/7 oz/small **can of pineapple pieces in natural juice**

15 ml/1 tbsp **tomato purée (paste)**

1 x 400 g/14 oz/large **can of chopped tomatoes**

150 ml/¼ pint/⅔ cup **beef stock**

Salt and freshly ground black pepper

30 ml/2 tbsp **chopped fresh coriander (cilantro)** or **parsley** (optional)

1   Heat the oil in a frying pan and cook the beef for 3–4 minutes, turning frequently until browned on all sides. Lift out the beef with a slotted spoon, leaving the fat and juices behind and transfer to the ceramic cooking pot.

2   Add the onions to the pan and cook for about 5 minutes, stirring occasionally until just beginning to brown. Sprinkle over the curry powder or stir in the paste and cook for a further minute.

3   Stir in the vinegar and jam, followed by the pineapple pieces and their juice, tomato purée, the chopped tomatoes and stock. Season with salt and pepper and heat until steaming, but not boiling. Pour over the beef, then cover with the lid.

4   Cook on High for 3–4 hours or on Low for 6–8 hours or until the beef is very tender.

5   Sprinkle with the herbs, if using and serve straight away with steamed basmati rice or warmed naan bread.

Tip
• Bought or home-made cucumber raita or ready-cooked popadoms are delicious served with this mild curry.

braised beef with honey

4

25 MINS

3-4 hrs HIGH

jacket (baked) or mashed potatoes and steamed seasonal greens

Chef's note

A hint of warmth from ginger and the sweetness of honey will make this dish a firm family favourite. You can use any kind of honey or wine vinegar.

25 g/1 oz/¼ cup **plain (all-purpose) flour**

10 ml/2 tsp **ground ginger**

Salt and freshly ground black pepper

700 g/1½ lb lean **braising or chuck steak**, trimmed and cut into 5 cm/2 in cubes

30 ml/2 tbsp **sunflower oil**

2 **onions**, sliced

15 ml/1 tbsp **grated fresh or bottled root ginger** or 2.5 ml/½ tsp ginger purée (paste)

1 **garlic clove**, crushed or 5 ml/1 tsp garlic purée (paste)

1 x 200 g/7 oz/small **can of chopped tomatoes**

15 ml/1 tbsp **honey**

15 ml/1 tbsp **wine vinegar**

15 ml/1 tbsp **Worcestershire sauce**

250 ml/8 fl oz/1 cup boiling **beef stock**

1 x 400 g/14 oz/large **can of red kidney beans**, drained and rinsed

1   Season the flour with the ground ginger and salt and pepper and coat the beef with seasoned mixture. Heat 15 ml/1 tbsp of the oil in a frying pan and fry the beef, turning frequently, until browned all over. Transfer to the ceramic cooking pot.

2   Heat the remaining oil in the frying pan and cook the onions for 5 minutes or until beginning to brown and soften. Stir in the fresh or bottled root ginger and garlic and cook for a further minute.

3   Add the chopped tomatoes, honey, wine vinegar and Worcestershire sauce to the pan. Heat gently for a minute, stirring until everything is combined, then pour over the beef. Add the stock to the ceramic cooking pot.

4   Give the mixture a quick stir, then cover with the lid and cook on High for 3–4 hours or Low for 6–8 hours or until the beef is very tender. Serve straight away with jacket or mashed potatoes and steamed seasonal greens.

Tip

• This casserole freezes well. Cool completely, then transfer to a freezer container and freeze for up to 2 months. Allow to defrost in the refrigerator overnight. To serve, heat gently in a saucepan and allow to bubble for about 5 minutes.

devilled meatballs

4

30 MINS

**20 mins HIGH +
3-5 hrs LOW**

spaghetti or noodles

Chef's note

Cooked on a bed of carrots and apple in a sweet and spicy sauce, these meatballs have a fresh and fruity flavour. The inclusion of soaked bread is a traditional touch that keeps the meatballs moist and tender.

50 g/2 oz crustless **white or wholemeal (whole wheat) bread**

2.5 ml/½ tsp **dried mixed herbs**

45 ml/3 tbsp **milk**

30 ml/2 tbsp **olive oil**

1 **red onion**, finely sliced

1 **garlic clove**, crushed or 5 ml/ 1 tsp garlic purée (paste)

10 ml/2 tsp **Dijon mustard**

15 ml/1 tbsp **Worcestershire sauce**

15 ml/1 tbsp **sweet chutney**

1 x 400 g/14 oz/large **can of chopped tomatoes**

Salt and freshly ground black pepper

225 g/8 oz **carrots**, cut into thin sticks

1 large **cooking (tart) apple**, peeled, cored and diced

150 ml/¼ pint/⅔ cup boiling **beef stock**

450 g/1 lb lean **minced (ground) beef**

1   Crumble the bread into a bowl, sprinkle with the herbs, then pour the milk over. Leave to soak for about 10 minutes.

2   Meanwhile, heat 10 ml/2 tsp of the oil in a non-stick frying pan. Add the onion and cook gently for 5 minutes until beginning to soften.

3   Stir in the garlic, mustard, Worcestershire sauce, chutney and tomatoes. Season with salt and pepper. Heat for a few minutes until hot, then transfer to the ceramic cooking pot.

4   Scatter the carrots and diced apple over the sauce, then pour in the stock. Cover with the lid and switch on the slow cooker to High. Cook at this temperature for 20 minutes while you make the meatballs.

5   Add the beef to the soaked bread and season generously with salt and pepper. Mix together thoroughly then, using floured hands, shape into 20 small balls.

6   Wipe the frying pan clean with kitchen paper (paper towels) and heat the remaining oil over a moderate heat. Fry the meatballs until lightly browned all over.

7   Add the meatballs to the ceramic cooking pot, re-cover and switch to Low. Cook for a further 3–5 hours or until the meatballs and vegetables are cooked through and tender.

8   Serve on a bed of spaghetti or noodles.

italian-style oxtail casserole

4 | **25** MINS | **6-8** hrs LOW | boiled potatoes and carrots

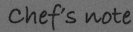

Chef's note

Oxtail has a wonderful rich flavour and really benefits from lengthy, moist, slow cooking. A high amount of fat surrounds the meat and bone, so make this casserole the day before and chill, so that you can remove the fat that rises to the surface. When reheated, the flavour of the casserole will be even better than when first cooked.

2 small **red onions**, thinly sliced

1.5 kg/3 lb **oxtail pieces**

15 ml/1 tbsp **olive oil**

50 g/2 oz **pancetta**, cubed

150 ml/¼ pint/⅔ cup **dry white wine**, preferably Italian

2 **garlic cloves**, crushed or 10 ml/2 tsp garlic purée (paste)

300 ml/½ pint/1¼ cups boiling **beef stock**

1 x 400 g/14 oz/large **can of chopped tomatoes**

Salt and freshly ground black pepper

Zest of half a **lemon**

1 Arrange the onion slices on the base of the ceramic cooking pot. Rinse the oxtail under cold running water, then pat it dry with kitchen paper (paper towels). Heat the oil in a frying pan and fry the pancetta for 3–4 minutes until golden. Lift out of the pan with a slotted spoon and transfer to the ceramic cooking pot, leaving all the fat behind.

2 Add the oxtail pieces to the pan and cook for 8–10 minutes, turning frequently until browned all over. Turn off the heat and pour in the wine. When the wine has stopped bubbling, transfer the oxtail pieces to the ceramic cooking pot using a slotted spoon, leaving the wine behind. Add the garlic to the pan and bring the wine back to the boil, stirring to mix in any sediment from the pan.

3 Pour the wine and garlic over the oxtail, then add the stock and chopped tomatoes. Season with salt and pepper, then add the lemon zest and cover with the lid and cook on Low for 6–8 hours or until the oxtail is very tender.

4 Leave to cool, then refrigerate for at least 4 hours or overnight if preferred. Remove and discard the fat that has risen to the top of the casserole. If liked, you can remove the pieces of meat from the bones, roughly chop and return to the casserole. Reheat in a saucepan until piping hot.

5 Serve with boiled potatoes and carrots.

oxtail casserole with olives

Chef's note

The flavour of oranges cuts through the richness of the oxtail and olives to add a unique flavour to this hearty casserole. Plan this dish well in advance so that you can chill it overnight and remove the fat. It reheats well and the taste improves with keeping.

1.5 kg/3 lb **oxtail pieces**

30 ml/2 tbsp **olive oil**

60 ml/4 tbsp **brandy**

1 **onion**, sliced

1 **garlic clove**, crushed or 5 ml/ 1 tsp garlic purée (paste)

175 ml/6 fl oz/¾ cup **dry white wine**

Finely grated zest and juice of 1 **orange**

Freshly ground black pepper

2 **bay leaves**

450 ml/¾ pint/2 cups boiling **beef stock**

75 g/3 oz/½ cup stoned (pitted) **black olives**

25 g/1 oz/2 tbsp **butter**, softened

25 g/1 oz/¼ cup **plain (all-purpose) flour**

1   Rinse the oxtail under cold running water, then pat it dry with kitchen paper (paper towels). Trim off any excess fat. Heat the oil in a heavy-based frying pan and fry the meat, turning frequently until it is browned all over.

2   Warm the brandy, pour over the oxtail and ignite the liquid by holding a match to the surface. When the flames have gone out, transfer to the ceramic cooking pot with a slotted spoon, leaving all the fat and juices behind. Add the onion and garlic and fry for 4–5 minutes or until beginning to brown. Turn off the heat and stir in the wine, orange zest and juice. Season with freshly ground black pepper.

3   Pour the mixture over the oxtail and tuck in the bay leaves. Pour over the stock, then cover with the lid and cook on Auto for 4–6 hours or Low for 6–8 hours or until tender.

4   Cool the casserole and chill overnight. The next day, remove the layer of fat from the top and discard.

5   Reheat the casserole in a saucepan with the olives. Cream the butter and flour together to make a *beurre manié*. Whisk this into the casserole a little at a time, until thickened. Bring to the boil and simmer for 2–3 minutes. Taste and adjust the seasoning if necessary. Discard the bay leaf.

6   Serve straight away with creamy polenta or couscous.

Tip
• A *beurre manié* – a paste of butter and flour – is a classic way of thickening a casserole and adds a glossy finish and richness. Add it a little bit at a time until the desired thickness is reached (you may not need it all), then simmer for 2–3 minutes to allow the flour to cook thoroughly.

ale-braised oxtail

| 4 | 25 MINS | 3-4 hrs HIGH | boiled or mashed potatoes and a green vegetable |

This simple casserole is enriched with ale, which adds both flavour and colour, and makes the meat meltingly tender. Don't be tempted to add more than the recommended amount, or the taste may be overpowering.

2 small **oxtails**, about 1.5 kg/3 lb in total

30 ml/2 tbsp **plain (all-purpose) flour**

Salt and freshly ground black pepper

30 ml/2 tbsp **sunflower oil**

2 **onions**, thinly sliced

150 ml/¼ pint/⅔ cup **brown ale**

10 ml/2 tsp **tomato purée (paste)**

225 g/8 oz **small carrots**, halved

225 g/8 oz **parsnips**, cut into large chunks

2 **bay leaves**

600 ml/1 pint/2½ cups **beef stock**

30 ml/2 tbsp chopped **fresh parsley**, to garnish

1   Trim the oxtails, rinse under cold running water, then pat dry. Cut into large pieces about 5 cm/2 in thick with a sharp knife and a cleaver (or ask your butcher). Trim off any excess fat.

2   Season the flour with salt and pepper, then use to coat the meat. Heat the oil in a large, heavy frying pan and fry the oxtail until well browned. Transfer to a plate and set aside.

3   Add the onions to the pan and gently fry for 5 minutes until just beginning to brown. Stir in the ale and tomato purée. Season with a little salt and pepper and turn off the heat.

4   Arrange some of the carrot halves and parsnips chunks in a single layer over the base of the ceramic cooking pot. Place the oxtail on top and any juices. Arrange the rest of the vegetables around the oxtail and tuck in the bay leaves.

5   Pour over the onion mixture, then just enough of the beef stock to cover. Put on the lid and cook on High for 3–4 hours or on Low for 6–8 hours or until tender.

6   Skim off any surface fat and discard the bay leaves.

7   Taste and adjust the seasoning, then stir in the parsley.

8   Serve with boiled or mashed potatoes and a green vegetable such as steamed, shredded cabbage.

creamy veal casserole

6 | **20** MINS | **3-4** hrs HIGH | hot buttered noodles and broad (fava) beans

900 g/2 lb **stewing veal**

30 ml/2 tbsp **plain (all-purpose) flour**

15 ml/1 tbsp **ground paprika**

1.5 ml/¼ tsp freshly grated **nutmeg**

Salt and freshly ground black pepper

30 ml/2 tbsp **sunflower oil**

2 **onions**, thinly sliced

2 **large carrots**, cut into quarters lengthways and sliced

4 **celery sticks**, thinly sliced

120 ml/4 fl oz/½ cup **dry white wine** or **vermouth**

300 ml/½ pint/1¼ cups **chicken stock**

120 ml/4 fl oz/½ cup **double (heavy)** or whipping cream

60 ml/4 tbsp **snipped fresh dill (dill weed)**

1 Cut the veal into 2.5 cm/1 in cubes. Combine the flour, paprika, nutmeg, salt and pepper in a bowl. Add the veal cubes and toss to lightly coat all the pieces.

2 Heat 15 ml/1 tbsp of the oil in a frying pan. Add the veal and cook, stirring for 2–3 minutes without browning. Transfer to the ceramic cooking pot.

3 Heat the remaining oil in the pan. Add the onions and cook for 5 minutes or until beginning to colour. Add the carrots and celery and cook for a further 2–3 minutes, stirring frequently. Add the wine or vermouth and bring to the boil, stirring.

4 Pour the vegetable mixture over the veal. Stir in the stock, cover with the lid and cook on High for 3–4 hours or Low for 6–8 hours.

5 Just before serving, stir in the cream and dill and cook on High for a further 15 minutes. Taste and adjust the seasoning if needed.

6 Serve straight away with hot buttered noodles and broad beans.

osso bucco

4

25 MINS

3-4 hrs AUTO

risotto alla Milanese, rice or buttered noodles

Chef's note

Osso bucco, which means 'bone with a hole', is a traditional veal stew from Milan that includes onions, leeks and tomatoes in white wine. It is usually served with a gremolata topping – a mixture of finely grated lemon zest, chopped parsley and garlic – which gives the dish a fresh finish.

25 g/1 oz/2 tbsp **unsalted (sweet) butter**

30 ml/2 tbsp **olive oil**

1 **large onion**, chopped

1 **large leek**, finely chopped

30 ml/2 tbsp **plain (all-purpose) flour**

Salt and freshly ground black pepper

4 large portions of **veal shin**, hind cut

300 ml/½ pint/1¼ cups **dry white wine**

150 ml/¼ pint/⅔ cup **chicken or vegetable stock**

1 x 200 g/7 oz/small **can of chopped tomatoes**

For the gremolata:

Finely grated zest of 1 **lemon**

30 ml/2 tbsp chopped **fresh parsley**

1 **garlic clove**, very finely chopped

1   Melt the butter and 10 ml/2 tsp of the oil in a large, heavy-based frying pan over a moderate heat. Add the onion and leek and cook for about 5 minutes, without browning. Transfer to the ceramic cooking pot.

2   Season the flour with salt and pepper and toss the veal pieces in it. Heat the remaining oil and fry the veal until it is well browned. Turn off the heat and transfer to the ceramic cooking pot. Swirl a little of the wine around the pan and stir to remove any cooking sediment. Pour over the veal, then pour over the rest of the wine, stock and tomatoes.

3   Cover with the lid and cook on Auto for 3–4 hours or on Low for 5–6 hours until the veal and vegetables are very tender.

4   For the gremolata, mix together the lemon zest, parsley and garlic.

5   Spoon the osso bucco on to warmed serving plates and sprinkle with the gremolata before serving. In Italy, osso bucco is always served with risotto alla Milanese but rice or buttered noodles make a good accompaniment.

Tip

• Buy thickly cut pieces of veal shin about 5 cm/2 in thick, so that they retain the marrow during cooking.

Although **lamb** cuts do not usually need tenderising, the **fragrant** flavour of the meat is **intensified** by slow cooking. Lamb is enjoyed around the world in a wealth of stews, **navarins** and tagines.

For simplicity, try a one-stage casserole such as Simple Irish Stew (see page 74) or Lancashire Hot-pot (see page 80), where the raw ingredients are layered without any pre-frying and the flavours slowly develop and mingle. You could also try Pot-roasted Shoulder of Lamb (see page 86); gentle slow cooking guarantees moisture and succulence. Lamb shanks are also very popular and make great individual servings.

Lamb comes from animals that are less than a year old and spring lamb from those that are aged between 5 and 7 months. Meat from older sheep is known as mutton and has a darker colour and stronger flavour. Although rarely available, it is excellent in casseroles and can be used instead of lamb in most recipes.

Lamb should be kept covered on a low shelf in the refrigerator. Pre-packed meat can be left in its packaging and used by the date given on the packet. When buying loose meat and chops, use within 2–3 days; larger cuts should keep for up to 4 days; your butcher will advise you.

lamb & barley stew

4-6 **30 MINS** **4-6 hrs AUTO** new potatoes and peas

Chef's note

Barley and root vegetables such as carrots and swede, make natural partners for lamb. In this warming winter stew, the barley adds to the flavour and texture as well as thickening the sauce to make a healthy satisfying meal.

30 ml/2 tbsp **sunflower oil**

2 **smoked streaky bacon** rashers (slices), rinded and chopped

15 g/½ oz/1 tbsp **butter**

1 **large onion**, chopped

30 ml/2 tbsp **plain (all-purpose) flour**

Salt and freshly ground black pepper

1 kg/2¼ lb boned **leg or shoulder of lamb**, trimmed and cut into 2.5 cm/1 in cubes

4 **carrots**, cut into 2.5 cm/1 in chunks

175 g/6 oz **swede (rutabaga)**, cut into 2.5 cm/1 in chunks

2 **celery sticks**, thickly sliced

30 ml/2 tbsp **pearl barley**

5 ml/1 tsp chopped **fresh thyme**

1 **bay leaf**

450 ml/¾ pint/2 cups boiling **lamb or vegetable stock**

1   Heat 15 ml/1 tbsp of the oil in a frying pan and fry the bacon for a minute or so until lightly browned. Remove with a slotted spoon and place in the ceramic cooking pot, leaving any fat behind in the pan.

2   Add the butter and onion to the frying pan and gently cook over a medium heat for 5 minutes until beginning to brown. Remove and add to the bacon in the cooking pot.

3   Season the flour with salt and pepper and toss the lamb in the mixture. Heat the remaining oil in the frying pan and fry the lamb until well browned on all sides. Add to the cooking pot.

4   Add the carrots, swede, celery, barley, thyme, bay leaf and stock. Season with salt and pepper. Cover with the lid and cook on Auto for 4–6 hours or on Low for 6–8 hours or until the lamb and vegetables are really tender.

5   Remove the thyme and bay leaf. Taste and adjust the seasoning if necessary.

6   Serve with boiled or steamed new potatoes and peas.

Tip
• Use smoked bacon lardons instead of the streaky bacon, if you prefer.

braised lamb shanks

4   **25 MINS**   **4½-6½ hrs LOW**   **sauté potatoes and a green vegetable**

Chef's note

Lamb shanks are full of flavour and each shank is the perfect individual portion. Here, a dash of balsamic condiment adds depth and a rich colour to the sauce.

4 **lamb shanks**

30 ml/2 tbsp **olive oil**

A few sprigs of **fresh rosemary**

2 **garlic cloves**, cut into slivers

Salt and freshly ground black pepper

1 **onion**, chopped

4 **carrots**, diced

2 **celery sticks**, thinly sliced (optional)

5 ml/1 tsp dried **Mediterranean herbs**, **thyme** or **oregano**

30 ml/2 tbsp **balsamic vinegar**

1 **bay leaf**

350 ml/12 fl oz/1⅓ cups boiling **lamb or vegetable stock**

1 x 400 g/14 oz/large **can of chopped tomatoes**

1 x 400 g/14 oz/large **can of cannellini beans**

1   Remove any excess fat from the lamb shanks. Heat the oil in a large frying pan, add the lamb shanks and brown on all sides. Lift out on to a board, leaving the fat behind in the pan.

2   With the tip of a sharp knife, make deep cuts all over the lamb shanks and insert a small sprig of rosemary and a sliver of garlic into each cut. Season with salt and pepper. Place in the ceramic cooking pot and switch on the slow cooker to Low.

3   Add the onion to the frying pan (there should be plenty of oil left; if not add a little more) and cook for 5 minutes, stirring frequently. Stir in the carrots and celery and cook for 2 more minutes. Turn off the heat and stir in the dried herbs and balsamic condiment. Spoon over and between the lamb shanks. Tuck in the bay leaf.

4   Pour the stock and chopped tomatoes over the meat and vegetables. If necessary, add a little more stock, so that the lamb shanks are just covered. Cover and cook for 4–6 hours or until the lamb and vegetables are tender. Skim off any fat that has risen to the top.

5   Drain the beans in a sieve (strainer) and rinse with boiling water (this will shorten the time that they take to heat through). Add to the slow cooker and cook for a further 30 minutes. Discard the bay leaf.

6   Spoon on to warmed plates and serve at once with sauté potatoes and a green vegetable.

Tip

• Balsamic vinegar is made in Modena in northern Italy. It is rich, dark and mellow and has a unique flavour, so don't use ordinary vinegar as a substitute in this dish.

lamb & apricot tagine

4 **25** MINS **4-6** hrs LOW COUSCOUS

Chef's note

While this isn't an authentic Moroccan tagine recipe, it does contain all the essential flavourings including cumin, cinnamon, lemon juice and a little harissa. The dish is named after the conical earthenware pot that cooks on gentle, even heat, allowing almost no moisture to escape. A slow cooker provides the perfect alternative.

1 **onion**, chopped

1 **garlic clove**, crushed or 5 ml/ 1 tsp garlic purée (paste)

2.5 ml/½ tsp **dried thyme** or mixed herbs

5 ml/1 tsp **harissa paste**

30 ml/2 tbsp **sun-dried tomato purée (paste)**

600 ml/1 pint/2½ cups very hot (not boiling) **vegetable or lamb stock**

450 g/1 lb boneless **cubed lamb**

5 ml/1 tsp **ground cumin**

5 ml/1 tsp **ground turmeric**

5 ml/1 tsp **ground cinnamon**

100 g/4 oz/⅔ cup **no-need-to-soak dried apricots**, quartered

Salt and freshly ground black pepper

30 ml/2 tbsp chopped **fresh or frozen coriander (cilantro)**

25 g/1 oz/¼ cup **toasted flaked (slivered) almonds**, to garnish (optional)

1   Put the onion, garlic and dried herbs into the ceramic cooking pot. Blend together the harissa paste, tomato purée and stock and pour over the onion mixture.

2   Cover with the lid and switch on the slow cooker to Low. Leave for 3–4 minutes while measuring and preparing the remaining ingredients.

3   Put the lamb in a bowl and sprinkle the cumin, turmeric and cinnamon over. Mix together to coat the cubes evenly in the spice mixture. Add to the cooking pot with the apricots and season with salt and pepper. Cover with the lid and cook for 4–6 hours or until the lamb is really tender.

4   Stir in the coriander and adjust the seasoning if necessary.

5   Serve the lamb with the toasted almonds sprinkled over. Couscous makes an excellent accompaniment.

Tip
• Widely used in North African and Middle Eastern cuisine, harissa is a hot aromatic paste made from chillies and other spices and herbs. Once opened, a jar will keep in the fridge for up to six weeks.

simple irish stew

4 | 25 MINS | 5-7 hrs LOW | peas or green beans

4 boneless lean **lamb leg steaks**, about 150 g/5 oz each

1 **large onion**, thinly sliced

5 ml/1 tsp **fresh or frozen thyme leaves** or a pinch of dried thyme

Salt and freshly ground black pepper

900 g/2 lb **potatoes**, thinly sliced

4 **carrots**, sliced

1 **bay leaf**

600 ml/1 pint/2½ cups hot **lamb, mild beef or vegetable stock**

1   Trim any excess fat from the lamb steaks and cut each into four pieces. Arrange the onion slices on the bottom of the ceramic cooking pot. Season with a little thyme and salt and pepper.

2   Add the following layers, seasoning between each layer with a little thyme and salt and pepper as you go: potato slices, followed by a layer of carrots and the bay leaf, then finish with any remaining potatoes. Finally top with the meat.

3   Pour the stock over the meat, adding a little more if necessary so that the meat is just covered. Cover the slow cooker with the lid and cook on Low for 5–7 hours or until the meat and vegetables are very tender. Discard the bay leaf.

4   Serve with an extra vegetable such as peas or green beans.

Tip
- Although cooking the meat on top of the potatoes sounds unusual, it reflects the amount of time for each raw ingredient to cook. Meat takes less time than vegetables, so is placed furthest away from the heat source, which is under the base of the ceramic cooking pot.

lamb with dill

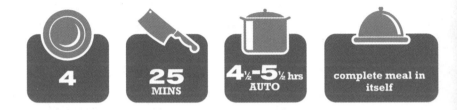

4

25 MINS

4½-5½ hrs AUTO

complete meal in itself

This recipe has a springtime feel, with its baby new potatoes, carrots and petits pois. The dill sauce is sharpened with a dash of lemon juice and thickened at the end of cooking by whisking in a mixture of egg yolk and cream (making it unsuitable for vulnerable groups). The vegetables make this a complete meal in itself.

700 g/1½ lb lean boneless **lamb**, cut into 2.5 cm/1 in cubes

4 sprigs of **fresh dill (dill weed)**, plus 45 ml/3 tbsp chopped

1 **bay leaf**

750 ml/1¼ pints/3 cups **hot lamb or vegetable stock**

10 ml/2 tsp **lemon juice**

225 g/8 oz **small shallots**, unpeeled

15 ml/1 tbsp **olive oil**

225 g/8 oz **baby carrots**, scraped

350 g/12 oz **baby new potatoes**, washed (leave unpeeled)

Salt and white pepper

150 g/5 oz **petits pois**, thawed if frozen

5 ml/1 tsp **cornflour (cornstarch)**

1 **egg yolk**

75 ml/5 tbsp **single (light) cream**

1   Put the lamb in the ceramic cooking pot with the sprigs of dill and the bay leaf. Pour the stock and lemon juice over, cover with the lid and switch on the slow cooker to Auto or High. Cook for 20 minutes.

2   Meanwhile, put the shallots in a heatproof bowl and pour over enough boiling water to cover. Leave for 10 minutes, then drain and peel off the skins when cool enough to handle.

3   Heat the oil in a frying pan, add the whole shallots and gently cook for 6–7 minutes, stirring frequently, or until just beginning to colour.

4   Skim the surface of the lamb mixture, then remove and discard the sprigs of dill. Add the shallots, carrots, potatoes and seasoning.

5   Leave the slow cooker on Auto or reduce the temperature to Low and cook for a further 4–5 hours, adding the petits pois 20 minutes before the end of the cooking time. Turn off the slow cooker. Remove the bay leaf.

6   Blend together the cornflour and egg yolk in a small bowl until smooth, then gradually mix in the cream and chopped dill. Stir in a few tablespoonfuls of the hot stock from the slow cooker, then return this mixture to the slow cooker in a thin stream, stirring all the time.

7   Serve at once.

aromatic lamb curry

4 | **30 MINS** | **5-7 hrs LOW** | low-fat natural (plain) yoghurt and chopped fresh coriander (cilantro)

Chef's note

Known in India as Kashmiri tamatari ghosht, this delicious dish is relatively low in fat. It already contains potatoes so there's no need to serve it with anything else – although warm Indian-style bread makes a great accompaniment.

30 ml/2 tbsp **sunflower oil**

700 g/1½ lb lean boneless **lamb**

5 ml/1 tsp **cumin seeds**

1 **onion**, thinly sliced

5 ml/1 tsp **ground turmeric**

2 **whole cloves** (optional)

2.5 ml/½ tsp **ground cinnamon**

1 **bay leaf**

2 **garlic cloves**, crushed or 10 ml/2 tsp garlic purée (paste)

15 ml/1 tbsp **freshly grated** or bottled ginger

350 g/12 oz **potatoes**, cut into chunks

1 x 400 g/14 oz/large **can of chopped tomatoes**

300 ml/½ pint/1¼ cups hot **lamb or vegetable stock**

Salt and freshly ground black pepper

1 Heat 15 ml/1 tbsp of the oil in a heavy-based frying pan and fry the lamb for 4–5 minutes or until lightly browned. Transfer to the ceramic cooking pot.

2 Heat the remaining oil in the pan, then sprinkle in the cumin seeds. When they start to pop, add the onion, turmeric, cloves, if using, cinnamon and bay leaf and cook gently for 2–3 minutes.

3 Stir in the garlic and ginger and cook for a few seconds more. Transfer to the ceramic cooking pot and switch on the slow cooker to Low.

4 Stir in the potato chunks, tomatoes and stock, then season with salt and pepper. Cover with the lid and cook for 5–7 hours or until the lamb and vegetables are very tender. Remove the bay leaf.

5 Serve the lamb curry drizzled with yoghurt and scattered with chopped coriander.

Tip
- You can keep a pot of coriander on the windowsill to snip whenever you need it.

lancashire hot-pot

Chef's note

Good, honest food! The meat and vegetables of this tasty dish are never browned first and the dish relies on long slow cooking to bring out all the flavours. If you use a food processor to slice the potatoes and onions, this dish can be prepared in a minimal amount of time.

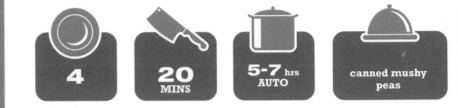

4

20 MINS

5-7 hrs AUTO

canned mushy peas

8 **middle neck or loin lamb chops**, about 900 g/2 lb in total

900 g/2 lb **potatoes**, thinly sliced

2 **onions**, sliced

2 **carrots**, sliced

1 **leek**, trimmed and sliced

5 ml/1 tsp **dried mixed herbs**

Salt and freshly ground black pepper

450 ml/¾ pint/2 cups hot **lamb or beef stock**

1 Trim the lamb chops of excess fat. Place a layer of sliced potatoes in the base of the ceramic cooking pot and top with some of the sliced onions, carrots and leek. Sprinkle with some dried herbs and salt and pepper.

2 Place four of the chops on top, then repeat the layers of potatoes, vegetables and seasoning and top with the remaining chops. Finish with a generous layer of potatoes.

3 Pour over the stock, then cover with the lid and switch the slow cooker to High or Auto. Cook for 1 hour.

4 Reduce the temperature to Low or leave on Auto. Cook for a further 4–6 hours or until tender.

5 Serve with mushy peas, if liked.

Tips

- Although not included in a classic Lancashire hot-pot, you could add other vegetables as well, such as a handful of thickly sliced button mushrooms or a stick of celery.
- If your cooking pot is suitable for use under a grill (broiler) – check carefully in your slow cooker manual – you can brush the top layer of potatoes with melted butter and grill (broil) for 5 minutes or until lightly browned.

mediterranean lamb

4

25 MINS

5-6 hrs LOW

pitta bread and Greek-style yoghurt

Chef's note

This Greek-inspired dish contains chunks of tender lamb and aubergine in a rich tomato sauce flavoured with cumin. A spoonful of mint jelly gives the sauce a fresh herby flavour and adds just a hint of sweetness.

1 **red onion**, chopped

1 **garlic clove**, crushed or 5 ml/ 1 tsp garlic purée (paste)

5 ml/1 tsp **dried Mediterranean herbs** or oregano

5 ml/1 tsp **balsamic vinegar**

30 ml/2 tbsp **mint jelly**

250 ml/8 fl oz/scant 1 cup hot **lamb or vegetable stock**

1 **aubergine (eggplant)**, about 250 g/9 oz

10 ml/2 tsp **ground cumin**

450 g/1 lb ready-cubed boneless **lamb**

1 x 400 g/14 oz/large **can of chopped tomatoes**

Salt and freshly ground black pepper

1 Put the onion, garlic and dried herbs into the ceramic cooking pot. Add the balsamic vinegar and mint jelly to the stock and stir until the jelly has dissolved. Pour over the onion mixture, cover with the lid and switch on the slow cooker to Low. Leave for a few minutes while preparing and measuring the remaining ingredients.

2 Trim the ends off the aubergine and cut into cubes, about 2 cm/¾ in. Sprinkle the cumin over the diced lamb and toss to lightly coat.

3 Add the aubergine, lamb and chopped tomatoes to the cooking pot and season with salt and pepper. Stir everything together, then cover and cook for 5–6 hours or until the lamb is really tender. Taste the sauce and adjust the seasoning if necessary.

4 Serve topped with Greek-style yoghurt and accompanied with pitta breads.

braised lamb fillet

4

35 MINS

3-5 hrs LOW

sugar snap peas

Chef's note

Tender lamb fillets are sandwiched together with a moist stuffing that subtly flavours the meat as it cooks. Gently braising in a Marsala gravy ensures that the meat is very tender and makes this a memorable dish. Make sure that the lamb fillets will fit in the slow cooker before you start. If necessary, cut them in half and make two parcels.

2 even-sized **fillets of lamb**, about 550 g/1¼ lb in total

Salt and freshly ground black pepper

25 g/1 oz/2 tbsp **butter**

1 **onion**, finely chopped

50 g/2 oz/1 cup **fresh breadcrumbs**

40 g/1½ oz/⅓ cup **toasted flaked (slivered) almonds**

Finely grated zest of 1 **lemon** and 30 ml/2 tbsp **lemon juice**

30 ml/2 tbsp chopped **fresh parsley**

1 **small egg**, lightly beaten

15 ml/1 tbsp **sunflower oil**

15 ml/1 tbsp **plain (all-purpose) flour**

300 ml/½ pint/1¼ cups hot **lamb or vegetable stock**

60 ml/4 tbsp **Marsala** or sweet sherry

1   Trim the lamb fillets, flatten a little (place between sheets of greaseproof (waxed) paper and hit with a rolling pin) and season lightly.

2   Melt the butter in a frying pan and gently cook the onion for 10 minutes until soft, stirring occasionally. Turn off the heat and stir in the breadcrumbs. Finely crush half the toasted almonds and stir in with the lemon zest, parsley and egg. Spread the stuffing over one piece of lamb, then cover with the second piece of lamb. Tie together with fine string.

3   Heat the oil in a frying pan and fry the parcel until browned all over. Transfer to the pot, leaving the juices in the pan.

4   Stir the flour into the pan juices and cook for 1 minute. Gradually add the stock and Marsala or sherry and simmer for 1 minute. Turn off the heat and stir in the lemon juice and season with salt and pepper. Pour over the lamb (but not directly on to the base of the cooking pot).

5   Cover and cook on Low for 3–5 hours or until very tender.

6   Lift out the lamb on to a board and leave to rest for a few minutes. Skim any fat from the gravy in the pot.

7   Cut off the string and carve the lamb into thick slices.

8   Serve with the gravy spooned over and scatter with the rest of the toasted almonds. Accompany with sugar snap peas.

pot-roasted shoulder of lamb

4-6 | **30** MINS | **4-5** hrs HIGH | warm crusty bread

Chef's note

Here a shoulder of lamb is studded with garlic and rosemary and cooked in a red wine and tomato sauce with flageolet beans. The recipe originates from Tuscany where this is a popular combination of flavours.

15 ml/1 tbsp **olive oil**

1.3 kg/3 lb **lamb shoulder**, trimmed, boned and tied

3 **garlic cloves**

12 small **fresh rosemary sprigs**

2 **smoked streaky bacon** rashers (slices), rinded and chopped

1 **onion**, chopped

2 **carrots**, chopped

2 **celery sticks**, chopped

1 **leek**, chopped

150 ml/¼ pint/⅔ cup **red wine**

Salt and freshly ground black pepper

300 ml/½ pint/1¼ cups hot **lamb or vegetable stock**

1 x 400 g/14 oz/large **can of chopped tomatoes**

1 x 400 g/14 oz/large **can of flageolet beans**, drained and rinsed

2 **bay leaves**

1 Heat the oil in a large frying pan and brown the lamb on all sides. Remove from the pan and cool for a few minutes.

2 Meanwhile, cut the garlic cloves into quarters. Make 12 deep incisions all over the lamb and push a piece of garlic and a rosemary sprig into each.

3 Add the bacon, onion, carrots, celery and leek to the frying pan. Fry for 5 minutes over a high heat, stirring all the time, until the bacon and vegetables are lightly browned. Turn off the heat and stir in the red wine.

4 Tip about half of the mixture into the ceramic cooking pot, then carefully place the lamb on top. Season with salt and pepper. Stir the stock, chopped tomatoes and beans into the remaining mixture and carefully pour around the lamb.

5 Tuck the bay leaves into the mixture, then cover with the lid and cook on High for 4–5 hours or until the lamb is cooked through and tender.

6 Remove the lamb from the pot and place on a board. Cover with foil and leave to rest for 10 minutes, before removing the string and carving. Skim any fat from the surface of the vegetables and discard the bay leaves.

7 Serve the lamb and vegetables with crusty bread.

Tip
• Flageolet beans have a delicate creamy flavour, but if you prefer, butter (lima) beans or cannellini beans may be used instead.

lamb ragù

Chef's note

A cross between a casserole and a thick meaty sauce, *ragù d'agnello* is perfect spooned on top of tagliatelle or other ribbon pasta. It's sometimes made with minced lamb but lamb fillet is much leaner.

4

30 MINS

5-7 hrs LOW

tagliatelle

700 g/1½ lb **lamb fillet**

30 ml/2 tbsp **plain (all-purpose) flour**

15 ml/1 tbsp **sunflower oil**

1 **large onion**, chopped

2 **small leeks**, sliced

2 **garlic cloves**, crushed or 10 ml/2 tsp garlic purée (paste)

1 x 400 g/14 oz/large **can of chopped tomatoes**

15 ml/1 tbsp **sun-dried tomato purée (paste)**

5 ml/1 tsp **dried thyme** or mixed herbs

150 ml/¼ pint/⅔ cup hot **lamb, beef or vegetable stock**

1 **small butternut squash**, cut into small cubes

Salt and freshly ground black pepper

1   Trim the lamb, then cut into small cubes about 1 cm/½ in. Toss in the flour, reserving any excess.

2   Heat the oil in a frying pan over a moderately hot heat and fry the lamb for 5 minutes, stirring often until browned all over. Transfer to the ceramic cooking pot.

3   Add the onion and leeks to the pan and cook for 5 minutes, stirring often. Stir in the garlic and cook for a few seconds, then sprinkle over any remaining flour from the lamb coating and stir.

4   Add the chopped tomatoes, tomato purée and herbs and heat until steaming hot, but not boiling. Carefully pour over the meat.

5   Pour in the stock and stir in the butternut squash, salt and pepper. Switch on the slow cooker to Low, cover with the lid and cook for 5–7 hours or until the lamb and vegetables are very tender.

6   Serve with tagliatelle.

navarin of lamb

4 | **30** MINS | **4-6** hrs LOW | spring (collard) greens and French bread

Chef's note

This classic French stew is made in the spring to celebrate the new season's lamb and young vegetables. Here it is prepared with lean leg of lamb but you can make it with best end lamb chops if you prefer.

175 g/6 oz **button (pearl) onions**, unpeeled

30 ml/2 tbsp **olive oil**

450 g/1 lb lean boneless **leg of lamb**, cut into cubes

1 **onion**, chopped

2 **garlic cloves**, crushed or 10 ml/2 tsp garlic purée (paste)

150 ml/¼ pint/⅔ cup **dry white wine**

1 **bay leaf**

900 g/2 lb **baby new potatoes**, scrubbed (unpeeled)

225 g/8 oz **baby carrots**

225 g/8 oz **baby turnips**, trimmed

Salt and freshly ground black pepper

400 ml/14 fl oz/1¾ cups hot **lamb or vegetable stock**

100 g/4 oz **frozen peas**, thawed

1   Put the onions in a heatproof bowl and pour over enough boiling water to cover. Set aside.

2   Meanwhile, heat 15 ml/1 tbsp of the oil in a frying pan. Add the lamb and fry for 5 minutes, turning frequently until browned all over. Transfer to the ceramic cooking pot with a slotted spoon, leaving any fat and juices behind in the pan.

3   Drain the onions and peel off the skins when cool enough to handle. Heat the remaining oil in the pan, then add the button and chopped onions and fry for 5 minutes.

4   Stir in the garlic and cook for 1 minute, stirring, then pour in the wine. Tip the mixture over the lamb.

5   Add the bay leaf, new potatoes, carrots and turnips to the cooking pot. Season with salt and pepper, stir, then pour over the stock. Cover with the lid and cook on Low for 4–6 hours or until the lamb and vegetables are tender.

6   Stir in the peas and cook for a further 15 minutes or until heated through. Discard the bay leaf.

7   Serve with steamed spring greens and crusty French bread.

spicy lamb with lentils

4

45 MINS

5-7 hrs LOW

chappatis and thick plain yoghurt

Chef's note

You'll need to grind or crush whole spices to make this dhansak-style curry but this doesn't take long and is well worth the effort. The result is a unique and fragrant dish, thickened with green lentils. Serve with classic Indian accompaniments such as chappatis and thick yoghurt.

6 **cardamom pods**

15 ml/1 tbsp **cumin seeds**

4 **black peppercorns**

30 ml/2 tbsp **sunflower oil**

450 g/1 lb lean boneless **neck fillet or leg of lamb**, cut into cubes

1 **onion**, sliced

2 **garlic cloves**, crushed or 10 ml/2 tsp garlic purée (paste)

Pinch of **dried chilli flakes** or 2.5 ml/½ tsp chilli powder

2.5 ml/½ tsp **ground cinnamon**

2.5 ml/½ tsp **ground ginger**

5 ml/1 tsp **ground turmeric**

450 ml/¾ pint/2 cups hot **lamb or vegetable stock**

175 g/6 oz **green lentils**, rinsed

1 x 200 g/7 oz/small **can of chopped tomatoes**

Salt and freshly ground black pepper

1 Remove the black seeds from the cardamom pots and crush with the cumin seeds and peppercorns in an electric grinder, with a pestle and mortar or using the end of a rolling pin on a board.

2 Heat 15 ml/1 tbsp of the oil in a large frying pan and fry the lamb for 5 minutes over a moderately hot heat until browned all over. Transfer the meat and juices to the ceramic cooking pot.

3 Add the remaining oil to the frying pan and fry the onion for 5 minutes over a high heat until beginning to brown. Turn down the heat and add the crushed garlic and all the spices. Cook for about 30 seconds, stirring. Turn off the heat.

4 Add a little of the stock to the pan and stir, then tip the mixture over the lamb. Stir in the rest of the stock, the lentils, chopped tomatoes, salt and pepper.

5 Cover with the lid and cook on Low for 5–7 hours or until the meat is very tender.

6 Serve with chappatis and thick plain yoghurt.

lamb with creamy mushroom sauce

4

20 MINS

5-8 hrs LOW

noodles or rice

Chef's note

Using a can of condensed mushroom soup is a really easy and inexpensive way to make a deliciously rich sauce. Add a few sliced mushrooms and no one will know you haven't spent ages making this casserole from scratch!

15 ml/1 tbsp **oil**

450 g/1 lb lean **lamb**, cubed

25 g/1 oz/2 tbsp **butter**, preferably unsalted (sweet)

2 **onions**, thinly sliced

1 **garlic clove**, crushed or 5 ml/1 tsp garlic purée (paste)

100 g/4 oz **mushrooms**, sliced

1 **red (bell) pepper**, seeded and sliced

300 g/11 oz/medium **can of condensed mushroom soup**

150 ml/¼ pint/⅔ cup hot **lamb or vegetable stock**

5 ml/1 tsp **dried mixed herbs**

Salt and freshly ground black pepper

1   Heat the oil in a large frying pan over a moderately hot heat and fry the lamb for 5 minutes, turning frequently until browned on all sides. Remove with a slotted spoon and transfer to the ceramic cooking pot.

2   Turn down the heat to moderate and add the butter to the pan. When melted, fry the onions for 5 minutes. Stir in the garlic and mushrooms and cook for 2 minutes, stirring.

3   Tip the onion and mushroom mixture into the ceramic cooking pot. Add the red pepper, soup, stock, herbs, salt and pepper. Gently stir everything together.

4   Cover with the lid and cook on Low for 5–8 hours or until the lamb and vegetables are tender.

5   Serve with noodles or rice.

blanquette d'agneau

Chef's note

In this classic dish the meat isn't browned so it retains its pale colour. The sauce is traditionally thickened towards the end of cooking with the addition of beurre manié and then enriched with a mixture of cream and egg yolk to give a silky texture. It's very rich, so serve with a simple accompaniment.

4

25 MINS

4-7 hrs LOW + **30** mins HIGH

boiled or steamed rice or new potatoes

2 **carrots**, sliced

1 **onion,** sliced

2 **celery sticks**, sliced

1 **bay leaf**

5 ml/1 tsp **dried thyme**

450 g/1 lb lean **shoulder of lamb**, diced

Salt and freshly ground black pepper

250 ml/8 fl oz/1 cup hot **lamb or vegetable stock**

25 g/1 oz/2 tbsp **butter**, softened

45 ml/3 tbsp **plain (all-purpose) flour**

1 **egg yolk**

150 ml/¼ pint/⅔ cup **single (light) cream**

30 ml/2 tbsp chopped **fresh or frozen parsley**

1   Put the carrots, onion and celery in the ceramic cooking pot. Add the bay leaf and sprinkle with the thyme. Place the meat on top and season with salt and pepper.

2   Pour over the stock, cover with the lid and cook on Low for 4–7 hours or until the lamb is tender. Turn up the slow cooker to High.

3   Blend together the softened butter and flour and add to the casserole in small knobs, whisking in each one before adding the next. Re-cover and cook for 15 minutes.

4   Blend together the egg yolk and cream. Stir into the casserole and reheat for a further 15 minutes or until steaming hot, but not boiling. Discard the bay leaf.

5   Sprinkle with the parsley before serving with boiled or steamed rice or new potatoes.

lamb & kidney hot-pot

4 | **30 MINS** | **4-7 hrs LOW** | **green beans**

Kidneys impart a distinct and rich flavour to this hot-pot, which is cooked with layers of sliced potatoes that soak up all the delicious juices, yet retain their shape in the slow cooker.

15 ml/1 tbsp **plain (all-purpose) flour**

Salt and freshly ground black pepper

450 g/1 lb lean **lamb**, cut into 2.5 cm/1 in cubes

4 **lambs' kidneys**, quartered and cored

30 ml/2 tbsp **oil**

1 **onion**, chopped

2 **carrots**, sliced

15 ml/1 tbsp **tomato purée (paste)**

15 ml/1 tbsp **Worcestershire sauce**

300 ml/½ pint/1¼ cups **lamb or vegetable stock**

700 g/1½ lb **potatoes**, scrubbed and sliced (unpeeled)

1 Season the flour with salt and pepper and use to coat the lamb and kidneys.

2 Heat 15 ml/1 tbsp of the oil in a large frying pan and fry the lamb and kidneys until browned all over. Lift out of the pan with a slotted spoon and transfer to a plate.

3 Add the remaining oil to the pan and fry the onion for 7–8 minutes until beginning to soften and brown. Stir in the carrots, tomato purée, Worcestershire sauce and stock. Bring to the boil, stirring, then turn off the heat.

4 Arrange half of the potato slices over the base of the ceramic cooking pot. Pour in the onion and carrot mixture, then top with the lamb and kidneys, adding any juices on the plate. Top with the rest of the potato slices.

5 Cover with the lid and cook on Low for 4–7 hours or until the potatoes and lamb are very tender.

6 Serve with green beans or another vegetable.

Tip
• If your ceramic cooking pot can be used under the grill (broiler), dot the potatoes with a little butter and place under a preheated moderate grill for a few minutes until browned.

pork

This light meat has a rich **flavour** and is very **versatile** in casseroles whether cut into bite-sized pieces or as lean loin steaks or chops. Whole cuts can be **pot-roasted** and pork products such as sausages and minced (ground) pork are also **fabulous** cooked in the slow cooker.

Bacon, ham and gammon are all cured cuts of pork and long slow cooking makes them very tender. You'll also find a tasty recipe using wild boar in this chapter.

Pork is widely eaten in Europe, Asia and South and Central America. Because of its rich taste and texture it goes well with fruity and acidic accompaniments such as apples, apricots and plums. Try recipes such as Pork with Apples and Cider (see page 106) or Fruity Pork Casserole (see page 110). Pungent herbs and spices such as rosemary, thyme and juniper are often added to pork dishes, such as Italian Sausage Stew (see page 130) and Wild Boar Ragù (see page 142). Throughout Europe cabbage is a popular vegetable accompaniment.

Store pork on a low shelf in the refrigerator, below any food that will be eaten raw. Keep pre-packed meat in its packaging and observe the dates given on the label. Minced pork can be kept for up to 2 days, while pork cuts and chops can be kept for 3 days.

pork & potato hot-pot

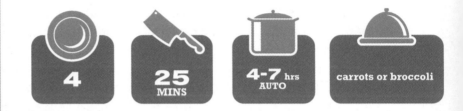

4 **25 MINS** **4-7 hrs AUTO** carrots or broccoli

Chef's note

The long, gentle cooking ensures that the pork is really tender and allows all the meat juices to be absorbed by the potatoes. This is the perfect dish for those chilly times of year when you know you'll want a good hot meal at the end of the day.

25 g/1 oz/2 tbsp **butter**

15 ml/1 tbsp **oil**

1 **onion**, finely sliced

1 **garlic clove**, crushed or 5 ml/ 1 tsp garlic purée (paste)

5 ml/1 tsp **dried mixed herbs**

900 g/2 lb **potatoes**, thinly sliced

Salt and freshly ground black pepper

750 ml/1¼ pints/3 cups hot **vegetable stock**

4 **chump or loin pork chops**

1 Use about a third of the butter to lightly grease the base and slightly up the sides of the ceramic cooking pot.

2 Heat the remaining butter and the oil in a frying pan and fry the onion for 7–8 minutes until softened. Stir in the garlic and cook for 1 minute. Stir in the herbs.

3 Spoon half the onion mixture into the base of the cooking pot and top with about half of the potato slices, seasoning with salt and pepper between the layers. Pour over a little of the stock to prevent the potatoes from turning brown.

4 Trim all the fat from the pork chops and place on top of the potatoes. Spoon the rest of the onion mixture around the chops, then top with the rest of the potatoes.

5 Pour over just enough of the stock to cover the potatoes, then cover and cook on Auto for 4–7 hours or on Low for 5–8 hours, until the meat and potatoes are tender.

6 Serve with carrots or broccoli, or another vegetable.

pork goulash

4 | **25** MINS | **4-6** hrs LOW | boiled or steamed potatoes

550 g/1¼ lb lean **pork**, trimmed and cut into cubes

30 ml/2 tbsp **plain (all-purpose) flour**

Salt and freshly ground black pepper

30 ml/2 tbsp **sunflower oil**

1 **large onion**, sliced

2 **garlic cloves**, crushed or 10 ml/2 tsp garlic purée (paste)

15 ml/1 tbsp **mild paprika**

5 ml/1 tsp **caraway** or **dill seeds**

150 ml/¼ pint/⅔ cup **red wine**

15 ml/1 tbsp **tomato purée (paste)**

250 ml/8 fl oz/1 cup **vegetable or chicken stock**

100 g/4 oz **whole baby button mushrooms**

1 **green (bell) pepper**, seeded and sliced

Soured (dairy sour) cream and **extra paprika**, to garnish

1   Toss the pork in the flour seasoned with salt and pepper. Heat 15 ml/1 tbsp of the oil in a large frying pan and fry the pork for 4–5 minutes, turning until browned all over. Transfer to the ceramic cooking pot with a slotted spoon.

2   Add the remaining oil to the pan and cook the onion for 5 minutes, stirring frequently. Stir in the garlic, paprika and caraway or dill seeds. Cook for 1 minute, stirring.

3   Pour in the wine and turn off the heat. Add the tomato purée and stir until blended. Season with salt and pepper, then pour over the pork. Add the stock and stir well. Cover with the lid and cook on Low for 3–5 hours.

4   Put the mushrooms and green pepper in a bowl and pour over just enough boiling water to cover. Leave for 5 minutes. Drain well, then stir into the casserole and cook for 1 more hour.

5   Serve topped with a few spoonfuls of soured cream and a sprinkling of paprika, accompanied by boiled or steamed potatoes.

Tip
- The mushrooms and pepper aren't essential to this dish and can be left out if you prefer; simply cook the casserole on Low for 4–6 hours.

pork with apples & cider

4 **25** MINS **3-6** hrs AUTO rice or new potatoes and a green vegetable

Chef's note

Pork lends itself to fruity sauces with a touch of tartness as they help to balance the richness of the meat. Thick slices of eating apple are used for this country-style recipe as they keep their shape.

30 ml/2 tbsp **plain (all-purpose) flour**

Salt and freshly ground black pepper

700 g/1½ lb lean **pork**, trimmed and cut into cubes

30 ml/2 tbsp **sunflower oil**

2 **small onions**, cut into thin wedges

2 **eating (dessert) apples**, such as Cox's, peeled, cored and cut into 8 wedges

300 ml/½ pint/1¼ cups **cider**

300 ml/½ pint/1¼ cups hot **vegetable stock**

1 **bay leaf**

15 ml/1 tbsp chopped **fresh sage** or 5 ml/1 tsp **dried sage** or **mixed herbs**

1   Season the flour with salt and pepper, then add the pork cubes and toss to coat.

2   Heat 15 ml/1 tbsp of the oil in a frying pan over a moderate heat, add the pork and cook for 2–3 minutes, turning frequently until browned on all sides. Transfer it to the ceramic cooking pot with a slotted spoon.

3   Heat the remaining oil in the pan, add the onions and fry gently for 5 minutes until almost soft. Stir in the apple, then turn off the heat. Pour in the cider and stir to loosen any sediment from the bottom of the pan. Pour the mixture over the pork.

4   Stir in the stock and herbs, cover with the lid and cook on Auto for 3–6 hours or on Low for 4–7 hours, or until the pork is really tender.

5   Remove the bay leaf and serve with rice or new potatoes and a green vegetable.

Tip
- Unsweetened apple juice can be used instead of cider if preferred.

apricot-stuffed pork fillet

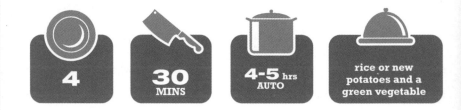

4

30 MINS

4-5 hrs AUTO

rice or new potatoes and a green vegetable

Chef's note

Apricots have a natural affinity with pork and this simple stuffing helps to keep the meat moist as it cooks. Wrapping the fillets with Parma ham gives a luxurious touch and makes it a great dinner-party dish.

25 g/1 oz/2 tbsp **butter**

2 **shallots**, finely chopped

10 ml/2 tsp **grated orange zest**

100 g/4 oz/⅔ cup **no-need-to-soak dried apricots**, finely chopped

25 g/1 oz/½ cup **fresh white breadcrumbs**

90 ml/6 tbsp **orange juice**

Salt and freshly ground black pepper

450 g/1 lb **pork tenderloin** (2 whole fillets), trimmed

4 slices of **Parma ham**

15 ml/1 tbsp **sunflower oil**

250 ml/8 fl oz/1 cup hot **vegetable stock**

1   Melt the butter and fry the shallots for 5 minutes until soft. Turn off the heat and stir in the orange zest, apricots, breadcrumbs, 25 ml/1½ tbsp of the orange juice, salt and pepper.

2   Make a pocket in the pork fillets by cutting them lengthways, about three-quarters of the way through. Open them up and place on a board. Cover the meat with a piece of lightly oiled baking parchment, then gently hit with a rolling pin to flatten the meat until it is slightly thicker than 5 mm/¼ in.

3   Spoon the stuffing along the middle of the fillets, then roll up to enclose the filling. Put the slices of Parma ham on the board, overlapping slightly so that the fat is on the outside. Place the fillets on top, roll the ham around and secure with wooden cocktail sticks (toothpicks).

4   Cut the fillets in half widthways. Heat the oil in a non-stick frying pan and lightly sear the fillets until the surface is just sealed, then place in the ceramic cooking pot. Pour in the remaining orange juice and the stock.

5   Cover with the lid and cook on Auto or High for 1 hour, then leave on Auto or reduce to Low and cook for a further 3–4 hours or until the meat is very tender. Turn off the slow cooker and leave for 10 minutes before slicing the meat.

6   Serve with rice or new potatoes and a green vegetable.

fruity pork casserole

4-6   **40** MINS   **4-6** hrs LOW   plain boiled or steamed rice

Chef's note

This casserole is inspired by the Mexican mole – a paste made from chillies, shallots and nuts – which is used to both flavour and thicken the sauce. It also contains dried fruit to sweeten and add texture to the final dish.

45 ml/3 tbsp **olive oil**

2 **onions**, roughly chopped

2 **garlic cloves**, crushed or 10 ml/2 tsp garlic purée (paste)

2 **red chillies**, seeded and roughly chopped

10 ml/2 tsp **ground coriander**

50 g/2 oz/½ cup **flaked (slivered) almonds**

2.5 ml/½ tsp **dried oregano**

Finely grated zest and juice of 1 **small orange**

300 ml/½ pint/1¼ cups **vegetable stock**

30 ml/2 tbsp **plain (all-purpose) flour**

Salt and freshly ground black pepper

700 g/1½ lb lean **pork**, trimmed and cut into cubes

250 ml/8 fl oz/1 cup **white wine** or **extra stock**

50 g/2 oz/⅓ cup **ready-to-eat prunes**, halved

50 g/2 oz/⅓ cup **no-need-to-soak dried apricots**, halved

1   Heat 25 ml/1½ tbsp of the oil in a frying pan and fry the onions over a low heat for 7–8 minutes until soft. Stir in the garlic, chillies, coriander, almonds and oregano. Cook, stirring, for 2 minutes. Turn off the heat and stir in the orange zest and juice.

2   Spoon the onion mixture into a food processor or blender. Add 60 ml/4 tbsp of the stock and process to a fairly smooth paste. Transfer to the ceramic cooking pot.

3   Season the flour with salt and pepper, then add the pork cubes and toss to coat.

4   Wipe the frying pan clean with kitchen paper (paper towels). Heat the remaining oil and fry the pork for 4–5 minutes, turning until brown all over. Transfer to the cooking pot with a slotted spoon.

5   Pour the remaining stock into the pan and stir over a low heat to loosen any sediment from the bottom of the pan. Pour the mixture over the pork. Add the white wine or extra stock, prunes, apricots, salt and pepper. Mix well.

6   Cover and cook on Low for 4–6 hours or until the meat is very tender.

7   Serve with plain boiled or steamed rice.

paprika pork

4 | **25** MINS | **5-7** hrs LOW | tagliatelle

chef's note

Paprika is the ground powder of dried red peppers and may be mild or slightly spicier, so check the label carefully. It gives this dish a rich, smoky flavour and vibrant colour. Raisins add a hint of fruity sweetness and go beautifully with paprika.

25 g/1 oz/2 tbsp **butter**

15 ml/1 tbsp **sunflower oil**

550 g/1¼ lb lean **pork**, trimmed and cut into cubes

2 **onions**, sliced

15 ml/1 tbsp **mild paprika**

30 ml/2 tbsp **plain (all-purpose) flour**

250 ml/8 fl oz/1 cup **vegetable or chicken stock**

15 ml/1 tbsp **tomato purée (paste)**

15 ml/1 tbsp **lemon juice**

Salt and freshly ground black pepper

1 x 400 g/14 oz/large **can of chopped tomatoes**

A handful of **raisins**

1. Melt half the butter and the oil in a frying pan and cook the pork over a moderately high heat for 4–5 minutes, until brown all over. Transfer to the ceramic cooking pot with a slotted spoon.

2. Add the remaining butter to the pan and fry the onions for 5 minutes until golden. Sprinkle over the paprika and flour and cook for 1 minute, then gradually add the stock and bring to the boil.

3. Stir in the tomato purée, lemon juice, salt and pepper. Pour the mixture over the pork.

4. Add the chopped tomatoes and raisins and stir. Cover with the lid and cook on Low for 5–7 hours or until the pork is very tender.

5. Serve with tagliatelle.

sweet & sour pork

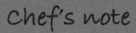

4 | 25 MINS | 3-4 hrs LOW | egg noodles or rice

Chef's note

This casserole has all the flavour of a stir-fry but without the need for last-minute cooking. By using lean and tender pork fillet and cooking on the Low setting, the meat remains moist and flavoursome and the vegetables retain a slightly crunchy texture.

350 g/12 oz **pork fillet**

15 ml/1 tbsp **sunflower oil**

100 g/4 oz **whole baby button mushrooms**

100 g/4 oz **baby sweetcorn**, halved lengthways

1 **red (bell) pepper**, seeded and sliced

1 x 220 g/7½ oz/small **can of water chestnuts**, drained and thickly sliced

1 x 225 g/8 oz/small **can of pineapple pieces in natural juice**

15 ml/1 tbsp **cornflour (cornstarch)**

10 ml/2 tsp **grated fresh or bottled ginger**

5 ml/1 tsp **Chinese five-spice powder**

15 ml/1 tbsp **dark soy sauce**

10 ml/2 tsp **sherry vinegar** or wine vinegar

10 ml/2 tsp **clear honey**

1 Trim away any visible fat from the pork and cut into 1 cm/ ½ in slices. Heat the oil in a non-stick frying pan over a high heat. Add the pork and cook for 2–3 minutes, turning the pieces until browned on both sides. Transfer to the ceramic cooking pot.

2 Add the mushrooms, sweetcorn, red pepper, water chestnuts and pineapple pieces to the pan. Blend the cornflour with 30 ml/2 tbsp of the pineapple juice, then stir in the rest of the juice.

3 Stir the ginger, five-spice powder, soy sauce, vinegar and honey into the pineapple juice. Add to the frying pan and stir over a moderate heat until thickened. Pour over the meat and vegetables in the cooking pot.

4 Stir well. Cover with the lid and cook on Low for 3–4 hours or until the pork is tender and the vegetables are cooked, but still slightly crunchy.

5 Serve with egg noodles or rice.

Tip
• Five-spice powder is made from ground star anise, fennel seeds, cloves, cinnamon and Sichuan pepper.

chinese pork with plums

4   **35 MINS**   **3-5 hrs LOW**   noodles or rice

chef's note

This is a delicious dish of lean pork loin steaks and vegetables cooked in a fresh and fruity plum sauce. It's ideal in late summer when plums are in season and inexpensive.

15 ml/1 tbsp **sunflower oil**

4 lean **pork loin steaks**, trimmed

700 g/1½ lb **ripe red plums**, such as Victoria

6 **spring onions (scallions)**, trimmed

1 **sweet potato**

1 **garlic clove**, crushed or 5 ml/ 1 tsp garlic purée (paste)

2.5 cm/1 in piece of **fresh root ginger**, peeled and grated or 15 ml/1 tbsp ginger purée (paste)

10 ml/2 tsp **soft light brown sugar**

15 ml/1 tbsp **dark soy sauce**

15 ml/1 tbsp **cider vinegar** or wine vinegar

30 ml/2 tbsp **dry sherry**

2.5 ml/½ tsp **Chinese five-spice powder**

60 ml/4 tbsp **vegetable or chicken stock**

Salt and freshly ground black pepper

1   Heat the oil in a frying pan over a moderately high heat. Pat the pork steaks dry on kitchen paper (paper towels). When the oil is hot, add to the pan and lightly brown on both sides. Turn off the heat.

2   Roughly chop the plums, cut the spring onions into 2 cm/¾ in lengths and the sweet potato into 1 cm/½ in cubes. Put in the ceramic cooking pot and mix together.

3   Place the chops on top of the plum mixture, tipping over any juices left in the pan.

4   Blend together the garlic, ginger, sugar, soy sauce, vinegar, sherry, five-spice powder and stock. Pour over the pork.

5   Cover with the lid and cook on Low for 3–5 hours or until the plums have cooked to a thick pulpy sauce and the pork and sweet potatoes are tender.

6   Taste the sauce and add a little more sugar or vinegar if needed, depending on the sweetness of the plums. Season to taste with salt and pepper.

7   Serve with noodles or rice.

Tip
• You can use red or white wine vinegar.

pork & madeira casserole

| 4 | 25 MINS | 4-7 hrs LOW | mashed potatoes and spring (collard) greens |

Chef's note

Madeira adds a wonderful rich flavour and subtle sweetness to this casserole. Medium-sweet sherry makes a good alternative, if you prefer.

175 g/6 oz **button (pearl) onions**, unpeeled

15 ml/1 tbsp **sunflower oil**

550 g/1¼ lb lean **pork**, trimmed and cut into cubes

25 g/1 oz/2 tbsp **butter**

100 g/4 oz **mushrooms**, thickly sliced

225 g/8 oz **carrots**, thickly sliced

2 **celery sticks**, thickly sliced

30 ml/2 tbsp **plain (all-purpose) flour**

450 ml/¾ pint/2 cups **vegetable stock**

60 ml/4 tbsp **Madeira**

2 **bay leaves**

Salt and freshly ground black pepper

1   Put the onions in a heatproof bowl and pour over enough boiling water to cover. Leave for 5 minutes.

2   Meanwhile, heat the oil and fry the pork for 4–5 minutes, turning until browned all over. Transfer to the ceramic cooking pot with a slotted spoon, leaving any fat and juices behind.

3   Drain the onions and peel off the skins when cool enough to handle. Melt the butter in the pan and cook the onions over a moderate heat until beginning to brown. Add the mushrooms, carrots and celery and cook for 2 minutes, stirring.

4   Sprinkle over the flour and stir in, then gradually add the stock. Bring to the boil, stirring until thickened. Turn off the heat and add the Madeira. Pour over the pork. Add the bay leaves and season with salt and pepper.

5   Cover with the lid and cook on Low for 4–7 hours or until the meat and vegetables are very tender. Discard the bay leaves.

6   Serve with creamy mashed potatoes and spring greens.

Tip
• Use pork fillet or less expensive ready-cubed casserole pork for this dish.

pork with braised red cabbage

4

30 MINS

5-7 hrs AUTO

sauté or creamy mashed potatoes

25 g/1 oz/2 tbsp **butter**

1 **large onion**, sliced

1 **small red cabbage**, cored and finely sliced

1 **cooking (tart) apple**, peeled, cored and thinly sliced

45 ml/3 tbsp **soft brown sugar**

2.5 ml/½ tsp **ground allspice**

1.5 ml/¼ tsp freshly grated **nutmeg**

60 ml/4 tbsp **red wine vinegar**

Salt and freshly ground black pepper

900 g/2 lb **pork shoulder**

120 ml/4 fl oz/½ cup **light vegetable stock or water**

30 ml/2 tbsp **redcurrant jelly (clear conserve)**

1 Melt the butter over a medium heat and fry the onion for 6–7 minutes, stirring often, until soft but not browned. Spoon half into the ceramic cooking pot.

2 Mix together the remaining onion mixture with the red cabbage, apple, sugar, spices, vinegar and salt and pepper in a large bowl.

3 Add most of the red cabbage mixture to the cooking pot, packing it tightly. Top with the pork, then add the rest of the cabbage mixture around the joint.

4 Pour in the stock or water, stir in the redcurrant jelly and cover with the lid. Cook on High or Auto for 1 hour, then leave on Auto or turn down the heat to Low and cook for a further for 4–6 hours or until the meat is tender.

Tip

• If you like crackling, score the rind before adding the pork shoulder to the slow cooker, then after cooking put the crackling under a hot grill (broiler) for a few minutes until browned and crisp.

pork & beans

4

20 MINS plus soaking time

4-7 hrs LOW

jacket (baked) potatoes or crusty bread

175 g/6 oz/1 cup **dried haricot (navy) beans**

4 **smoked streaky bacon** rashers (slices), rind removed and chopped

4 thin lean **pork chump chops**, about 600 g/1 lb 6 oz in total

10 ml/2 tsp **sunflower oil**

1 **onion**, chopped

250 ml/8 fl oz/1 cup **dark ale**

1 x 400 g/14 oz/large **can of chopped tomatoes**

15 ml/1 tbsp **Worcestershire sauce**

15 ml/1 tbsp **mild American or French mustard**

15 ml/1 tbsp **light soft brown sugar**

Salt and freshly ground black pepper

1 Put the haricot beans in a large saucepan and cover with cold water. Leave to soak for 8 hours, or overnight.

2 Drain and rinse the beans and return them to the saucepan. Cover with cold water and bring to the boil. Boil for 15 minutes, skimming off any surface scum, then turn off the heat and leave for a few minutes.

3 Fry the bacon in a non-stick frying pan for 3–4 minutes until lightly browned and most of the fat has run out. Transfer to the ceramic cooking pot with a slotted spoon, leaving the fat behind in the pan.

4 Add the pork chops to the pan and fry for about a minute on each side until browned. Remove and place on a plate.

5 Add the oil and onion to the pan and cook for 5 minutes or until beginning to soften and colour. Add the ale and simmer for a few seconds, then turn off the heat. Stir in the tomatoes, Worcestershire sauce, mustard and sugar.

6 Drain the beans and tip into the ceramic cooking pot. Arrange the pork chops on top, adding any juices on the plate. Pour over the onion and tomato mixture.

7 Cover with the lid and cook on Low for 4–7 hours or until tender. Season to taste with salt and pepper.

8 Serve with jacket potatoes or crusty bread.

boston baked beans

4   **20 MINS** plus soaking time   **7-8 hrs LOW**   mashed potatoes

Chef's note

The slow cooker was originally invented for making baked beans, so is perfect for cooking pulses. This is a classic dish made with a piece of salt pork; it always contains molasses, which gives the beans a dark colour and rich flavour.

175 g/6 oz/1 cup **dried haricot (navy) beans**

2 **whole cloves**

1 **onion**

1 **bay leaf**

45 ml/3 tbsp **tomato ketchup (catsup)**

15 ml/1 tbsp **black treacle (molasses)**

15 ml/1 tbsp **dark soft brown sugar**

10 ml/2 tsp **Dijon mustard**

250 ml/8 fl oz/1 cup **vegetable stock**

225 g/8 oz piece of **salt pork**

Freshly ground black pepper

1   Put the haricot beans in a large saucepan and cover with cold water. Leave to soak for 8 hours or overnight.

2   Drain and rinse the beans and return them to the saucepan. Cover with plenty of cold water and bring to the boil. Boil for 10 minutes, then skim, drain and tip into the ceramic pot.

3   Stick the cloves in the onion. Add it to the pot with the bay leaf, submerging in the beans.

4   Blend together the ketchup, treacle, sugar, mustard and stock and pour over the beans. Add a little more stock or water if necessary, so that the beans are just covered with liquid. Cover with the lid and cook on Low for 3 hours.

5   Near the end of cooking, put the salt pork in a pan of cold water. Bring to the boil and simmer for 2 minutes. Drain and leave for a few minutes, then score the rind with a sharp knife.

6   Push the salt pork, skin-side up, down into the beans. Re-cover and cook for a further 4–5 hours on Low or until tender.

7   Remove the pork and leave on a board until cool enough to handle. Discard the rind and fat, then slice the meat.

8   Skim off any fat from the top of the beans and remove the bay leaf. Stir in the pieces of meat and season with black pepper.

9   Serve with mashed potatoes.

bigos

 **25 MINS** plus soaking time

 **5-7 hrs** LOW

 jacket (baked) potatoes or rye bread

Chef's note

This rich winter stew is Poland's national dish and may be made with all pork, as here, or with a mixture of pork, venison and beef.

15 g/½ oz/¼ cup **dried porcini mushrooms**

450 g/1 lb lean boneless **pork**

225 g/8 oz **kielbasa**

30 ml/2 tbsp **plain (all-purpose) flour**

Salt and freshly ground black pepper

30 ml/2 tbsp **olive oil**

1 **onion**, sliced

450 g/1 lb **can or packet of sauerkraut**, drained and rinsed

1 x 200 g/7 oz/small **can of chopped tomatoes**

100 g/4 oz/⅔ cup **ready-to-eat stoned (pitted) prunes**

2 **whole cloves**

1 **bay leaf**

2.5 ml/½ tsp **dill seeds**

300 ml/½ pint/1¼ cups **vegetable or beef stock**

1   Put the mushrooms in a heatproof bowl, then pour over enough boiling water to cover. Leave to soak for 20 minutes, then drain well.

2   Meanwhile, cut the pork and kielbasa into 2.5 cm/1 in cubes, then toss together in the flour, seasoned with salt and pepper.

3   Heat 15 ml/1 tbsp of the oil and fry the meat for 4–5 minutes until browned all over. Lift out of the pan with a slotted spoon, leaving the fat behind and transfer to the ceramic cooking pot.

4   Add the rest of the oil to the pan and fry the onion for 5 minutes, until beginning to colour. Add to the cooking pot.

5   Drain the mushrooms and add to the cooking pot with the sauerkraut, chopped tomatoes, prunes, cloves, bay leaf, dill seeds and stock. Stir, then cover and cook on Low for 5–7 hours or until very tender. Discard the bay leaf.

6   Serve with jacket potatoes or rye bread.

Tip
• *Kielbasa* is a garlic-flavoured pork and beef sausage, but any similar European sausage may be used.

pork meatballs in red wine

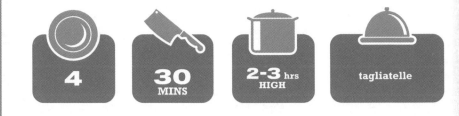

4

30 MINS

2-3 hrs HIGH

tagliatelle

25 g/1 oz/½ cup **wholemeal (whole wheat) breadcrumbs**

1 **small onion**, very finely chopped

450 g/1 lb lean **minced (ground) pork**

5 ml/1 tsp **dried mixed herbs**

Salt and freshly ground black pepper

15 ml/1 tbsp **olive oil**

175 g/6 oz **whole baby button mushrooms**

150 ml/¼ pint/⅔ cup **red wine**

150 ml/¼ pint/⅔ cup **vegetable or beef stock**

1 x 400 g/14 oz/large **can of chopped tomatoes**

1   Mix together the breadcrumbs, onion, pork, herbs and salt and pepper. Shape into 16 balls with slightly dampened hands.

2   Heat the oil in a frying pan and add the meatballs. Fry for 2 minutes, then add the mushrooms and cook for a further 2–3 minutes, turning frequently until the meatballs are brown all over.

3   Pour the wine, stock and tomatoes into the ceramic cooking pot. Season with salt and pepper and stir. Tip in the meatballs and mushrooms.

4   Cover and cook on High for 2–3 hours, Auto for 3–4 hours or Low for 4–6 hours, or until the meatballs are cooked through and tender.

5   Serve with tagliatelle.

Tip
- Minced beef, turkey or chicken may be used instead of minced pork.

italian sausage stew

4   **20** MINS   **4-7** hrs LOW   ciabatta or crusty bread

Chef's note

Variations of sausage and bean stew are found all over Europe. Some have lengthy ingredient lists, others are blissfully simple dishes, as here. Although spicy Italian sausages are suggested, you can use your favourite variety of plain pork sausage.

15 ml/1 tbsp **olive oil**

8 fresh spicy **Italian pork sausages**

50 g/2 oz **pancetta**, chopped (optional)

1 **onion**, thickly sliced

1 **garlic clove**, crushed or 5 ml/ 1 tsp garlic purée (paste)

1 **yellow (bell) pepper**, seeded and sliced

1 x 400 g/14 oz/large **can of chopped tomatoes**

1 x 400 g/14 oz/large **can of cannellini beans**, drained and rinsed

150 ml/¼ pint/⅔ cup **vegetable or beef stock**

2.5 ml/½ tsp **dried thyme** or **mixed herbs**

1 **bay leaf**

Salt and freshly ground black pepper

1   Heat the oil in a frying pan and add the sausages and pancetta, if using. Cook over a medium heat for 6–8 minutes, turning occasionally until lightly browned. Transfer to the ceramic cooking pot with a slotted spoon, leaving all the fat behind.

2   Drain off most of the fat, leaving just 15 ml/1 tbsp in the pan. Add the onion and fry for 5 minutes, then stir in the garlic and yellow pepper and cook for 1 minute.

3   Add the onion and pepper mixture to the ceramic cooking pot with the tomatoes, beans, stock, herbs and salt and pepper. Stir to combine.

4   Cover with the lid and cook on Low for 4–7 hours or until the beans and meat are tender. Remove the bay leaf.

5   Serve with ciabatta or crusty bread.

cumberland casserole

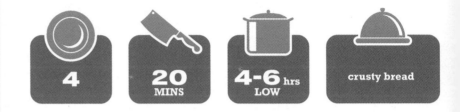

4   **20** MINS   **4-6** hrs LOW   crusty bread

Chef's note

Cumberland sausages are made to a traditional recipe and contain nothing but meat flavoured with herbs and spices. If you can't get these you can use any sausages with a high meat content.

15 ml/1 tbsp **sunflower oil**

450 g/1 lb **Cumberland sausages**, cut into bite-sized pieces

12 **small new potatoes**, scrubbed (unpeeled)

1 **onion**, sliced

2 **carrots**, chopped

1 **leek**, sliced

1 **garlic clove**, crushed or 5 ml/ 1 tsp garlic purée (paste)

15 ml/1 tbsp **plain (all-purpose) flour**

120 ml/4 fl oz/½ cup **red wine**

15 ml/1 tbsp **tomato purée (paste)**

250 ml/8 fl oz/1 cup hot **vegetable or beef stock**

Salt and freshly ground black pepper

1 Heat the oil in a frying pan, add the sausage pieces and brown for 3–4 minutes. Lift out of the pan with a slotted spoon, leaving all the fat behind and place in the ceramic cooking pot with the potatoes.

2 Add the onion to the pan and fry gently for 5 minutes. Stir in the carrots, leek and garlic and cook for 2–3 minutes.

3 Sprinkle the flour over and stir in, then add the red wine, a little at a time. Stir in the tomato purée, then turn off the heat.

4 Stir in the stock and season with salt and pepper. Pour over the sausage pieces, cover with the lid and cook on Low for 4–6 hours or until the potatoes and vegetables are tender.

5 Serve with crusty bread, if liked.

hungarian sausage stew

4

20 MINS

4-6 hrs LOW

seeded bread

Chef's note

As this dish slowly cooks, the potatoes soak up the flavour of the smoked sausage and paprika and thicken the stew, making it the perfect meal on a cold day.

15 ml/1 tbsp **sunflower oil**

1 **large onion**, chopped

400 g/14 oz **potatoes**, diced

10 ml/2 tsp **ground paprika**

2.5 ml/½ tsp **caraway seeds**

225 g/8 oz pack **smoked pork sausage**, thickly sliced

1 **red or yellow (bell) pepper**, seeded and sliced

1 x 400 g/14 oz/large **can of chopped tomatoes**

150 ml/¼ pint/⅔ cup **vegetable or beef stock**

Salt and freshly ground black pepper

1   Heat the oil in a frying pan and cook the onion for 6–7 minutes or until soft and beginning to brown.

2   Stir in the potatoes, then sprinkle over the paprika and caraway seeds. Cook for 2 minutes, stirring all the time.

3   Tip the mixture into the ceramic cooking pot. Add the sliced sausage, pepper slices, tomatoes and stock and season with salt and pepper. Stir, then cover with the lid. Cook on Low for 4–6 hours or until the vegetables are very tender.

4   Serve with buttered slices of seeded bread.

Tip
• There are several types of smoked pork sausage available, including garlic-flavoured and a reduced-fat version. All would be suitable for this recipe.

ham hock & lentil braise

4 | **20 MINS** + soaking time | **5-7 hrs** LOW + ½ hr HIGH | crusty white or wholemeal (whole wheat) bread

Chef's note

This simple rustic stew makes the perfect supper dish. A ham hock is braised until the meat is almost falling from the bone and creates a delicious stock for the lentil and vegetable mixture.

2 **unsmoked ham hocks or knuckles**, about 400 g/14 oz each

1 **onion**, chopped

About 750 ml/1¼ pints/3 cups hot **vegetable stock**

350 g/12 oz/2 cups **Puy lentils**, rinsed

2 **carrots**, diced

1 **bay leaf**

45 ml/3 tbsp chopped **fresh parsley**

Freshly ground black pepper

1   Put the ham hocks in a bowl and pour over enough cold water to cover. Leave to soak in a cool place or the refrigerator for at least 6 hours or overnight.

2   Put the onion in the ceramic cooking pot. Pour over about half the stock and switch on the slow cooker to Low.

3   Put the ham hocks on top of the onions, then tip the lentils and carrots around them. Tuck in the bay leaf, then pour in enough of the remaining stock to just cover the hocks.

4   Cover and cook for 5–7 hours, or until the meat and lentils are very tender.

5   Carefully remove the ham hocks to a board. Skim any surface fat off the lentils and remove the bay leaf. Re-cover the slow cooker with the lid and turn up the slow cooker to High.

6   Strip off the skin and fat from the ham. Remove the meat from the bone and shred it into small pieces. Return the pieces of ham to the slow cooker and stir in the parsley and a little freshly ground black pepper. Cook for a further 30 minutes. Remove the bay leaf.

7   Ladle into warmed bowls and serve with crusty bread.

gammon casserole

4-6

25 MINS

4-5 hrs HIGH

green beans

Chef's note

Gammon is sold raw as a whole or half gammon or as smaller cuts as used here, known as middle, corner and gammon hock. It can be quite salty, so taste before seasoning this casserole.

1.25 kg/2½ lb **middle gammon (ham)**

175 g/6 oz **button onions**

100 g/4 oz **button mushrooms**

225 g/8 oz **whole baby carrots**

225 g/8 oz **new potatoes**, scrubbed (unpeeled)

2 **celery sticks**, thickly sliced

2 **bay leaves**

1 sprig of **fresh thyme** or 2.5 ml/½ tsp dried thyme

250 ml/8 fl oz/1 cup **cider**

Salt and freshly ground black pepper

25 g/1 oz/2 tbsp **butter**, softened

25 g/1 oz/¼ cup **plain (all-purpose) flour**

1   If smoked, soak the gammon overnight in plenty of cold water, then drain well. Put the gammon in the ceramic cooking pot.

2   Put the onions in a heatproof bowl and pour over enough boiling water to cover. Leave for 5 minutes. Drain the onions and peel off the skins when cool enough to handle.

3   Add the onions, mushrooms, carrots, potatoes, celery, bay leaves and thyme to the ceramic cooking pot. Pour in the cider, then add just enough cold water to cover the gammon.

4   Switch the slow cooker to High, cover with the lid and cook for 1 hour. Skim off any scum from the surface, re-cover and cook for a further 3–4 hours or until the gammon is cooked and the vegetables are tender. Check once during cooking and skim the surface if necessary.

5   Carefully lift the gammon joint out of the slow cooker using large forks or slotted spoons. Cover with foil to keep warm and leave to rest for 10 minutes.

6   Meanwhile skim any fat off the top of the cooking liquid. Taste and season with pepper and a little salt if needed. Strain the stock into a saucepan, discarding the bay leaves and thyme sprig (if used) and keeping the vegetables.

7   Cream together the butter and flour. Bring the stock to the boil and whisk in the butter and flour mixture a little at a time until the desired thickness (see tip on page 59). Add the vegetables to the thickened sauce and reheat for a minute. Carve the gammon into thick slices.

8   Serve the gammon slices with the sauce and green beans.

gammon with sweet potatoes

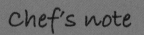

4   **35** MINS   **4-6** hrs LOW   broccoli

Chef's note

In this colourful modern casserole, cubes of gammon are cooked with chunks of sweet potato and pears, which complement the meat beautifully. Serve it with broccoli or another bright green vegetable.

15 ml/1 tbsp **sunflower oil**

2 **onions**, sliced

2 **firm cooking pears**, peeled, cored and thickly sliced

10 ml/2 tsp **lemon juice**

5 ml/1 tsp **soft light brown sugar**

10 ml/2 tsp **cornflour (cornstarch)**

15 ml/1 tbsp cold **water**

600 ml/1 pint/2½ cups hot **vegetable stock**

450 g/1 lb **sweet potatoes**, cut into 2 cm/¾ in chunks

2.5 ml/½ tsp **dried thyme**

A pinch of freshly grated **nutmeg**

Salt and freshly ground black pepper

400 g/14 oz lean boneless **gammon (ham)**, cut into 2 cm/¾ in chunks

1   Heat the oil in a frying pan and gently cook the onions for 7–8 minutes, until soft and beginning to colour. Stir in the pears and sprinkle over the lemon juice and sugar.

2   Blend the cornflour with the water, then stir in the stock. Pour over the onions and pears, bring to the boil, stirring until thickened, then turn off the heat.

3   Arrange the sweet potatoes in the ceramic cooking pot and sprinkle with the thyme, nutmeg, salt and pepper. Top with the gammon, then pour over the onion and pear mixture.

4   Cover with the lid and cook on Low for 4–6 hours or until the meat, sweet potatoes and pears are tender.

5   Serve with broccoli.

wild boar ragù

4 | **35 MINS + marinating time** | **5-7 hrs LOW** | **soft polenta (cornmeal)**

450 g/1 lb boneless **wild boar** for stewing

10 **juniper berries**, lightly crushed

2 **bay leaves**

2 **garlic cloves**, sliced

250 ml/8 fl oz/1 cup **red wine**

30 ml/2 tbsp **olive oil**

1 **onion**, chopped

2 **carrots**, chopped

2 **celery sticks**, sliced

10 g/¼ oz/2 tbsp **dried porcini mushrooms**

2.5 ml/½ tsp **dried mixed herbs**

Salt and freshly ground black pepper

1 x 200 g/7 oz/small **can of chopped tomatoes**

300 ml/½ pint/1¼ cups **beef stock**

1   Trim any fat from the wild boar and cut into bite-sized chunks. Put in a bowl with the juniper berries, bay leaves and garlic and pour over the red wine. Cover and marinate in the refrigerator for at least 6 hours or overnight if preferred.

2   Remove the meat from the marinade and pat dry with kitchen paper (paper towels). Heat 15 ml/1 tbsp of the oil in a frying pan and fry the meat over a moderately high heat for 2–3 minutes or until browned all over. Lift out of the pan with a slotted spoon and place on a plate.

3   Add the remaining oil to the pan and gently fry the onion for 5 minutes, then stir in the carrots and celery and cook for 2 more minutes. Tip into the ceramic cooking pot.

4   Rinse the porcini mushrooms under cold running water to remove any grit, then add these to the cooking pot. Put the meat and any juices from the plate on top of the vegetables. Sprinkle with the dried herbs, salt and pepper.

5   Pour over the chopped tomatoes and stock. Cover with the lid and cook on Low for 5–7 hours or until the meat is very tender.

6   Serve with soft polenta.

poultry & game

For succulence, flavour and **versatility**, poultry and game are hard to beat and there are many **delicious** cuts to choose from, including breasts, quarters and thighs. You have a huge **choice** of **wonderful** recipes here.

In this chapter you'll find more than a dozen chicken casserole recipes. Choose from well-known classics such as Coq au Vin (see page 148), Chicken Chasseur (see page 156) and Chicken Marengo (see page 150) to more modern casseroles including Chicken in Red Pepper Sauce (see page 162) and Chicken Parmigiana (see page 170). There are also plenty of turkey and duck recipes to try and game dishes that make the most of pheasant, pigeon (squab), guinea fowl and venison.

Buy poultry and game from a reliable source and refrigerate as soon as possible after purchase. If you can't cook within a day or two, poultry and game will keep for up to 3 months in the freezer; defrost overnight in the refrigerator and always check that it is thoroughly thawed before adding to the slow cooker. You should also make sure that larger pieces such as quarters and thighs are thoroughly cooked before serving by piercing at the thickest point; the juices should run clear and not be at all pink.

chicken cacciatora

Chef's note

In this famous Italian chicken classic, meaty chicken thighs are cooked with white wine and tomatoes until meltingly tender. 'Cacciatora' means 'the hunter's way' and the dish is certainly hearty and flavoursome.

15 ml/1 tbsp **olive oil**

8 **chicken thighs**, skinned and boned

1 **garlic clove**, crushed or 5 ml/ 1 tsp garlic purée (paste)

1 sprig of **fresh rosemary** and 1 sprig of **fresh thyme**, or 5 ml/1 tsp Mediterranean dried herbs

150 ml/¼ pint/⅔ cup **dry white wine**

150 ml/¼ pint/⅔ cup boiling **chicken stock**

1 x 200 g/7 oz/small **can of chopped tomatoes**

50 g/2 oz/⅓ cup stoned (pitted) **black olives**

25 g/1 oz **capers**, drained

Freshly ground black pepper

1   Heat the oil in a heavy, non-stick frying pan over a moderate heat, then add the chicken thighs. Cook for 2–3 minutes or until lightly browned, then turn over and cook for a further 2–3 minutes, adding the garlic for the last minute. Turn off the heat.

2   Transfer the chicken and garlic to the ceramic cooking pot and add the rosemary and thyme or dried herbs. Pour the wine into the frying pan and give it a stir (this will warm it a little and remove any remaining garlic and chicken juices). Tip over the chicken.

3   Add the stock, chopped tomatoes, olives and capers. Season with black pepper (you probably won't need any salt because the olives and capers are salty already).

4   Cover with the lid and cook for 3–5 hours on Auto or 2–3 hours on High, until the chicken is tender and thoroughly cooked. Discard the herb sprigs if used. Taste and adjust the seasoning if necessary, then spoon the casserole on to warmed plates.

5   Serve with ciabatta rolls and a green salad, if liked.

coq au vin

4

30 MINS, plus marinating time

4-6 hrs AUTO

new or sauté potatoes and a green vegetable

Chef's note

This is a well-known French dish in which the chicken is marinated overnight in red wine to both tenderise and give it extra flavour. Always choose a wine that you enjoy drinking rather than cheap 'cooking' wine that may spoil the taste of the finished dish.

4 **chicken quarters**, skinned

400 ml/14 fl oz/1¾ cups **red wine**, such as Burgundy

15 ml/1 tbsp **olive oil**

1 **onion**, chopped

2 **garlic cloves**, crushed or 10 ml/2 tsp garlic purée (paste)

225 g/8 oz **baby button mushrooms**

5 ml/1 tsp **dried thyme** or dried mixed herbs

5 ml/1 tsp **Dijon mustard**

300 ml/½ pint/1¼ cups **chicken stock**

Salt and freshly ground black pepper

30 ml/2 tbsp chopped **fresh or frozen parsley**

1   Place the chicken quarters in a dish in which they fit fairly snugly. Pour the wine over. Cover tightly and marinate in the refrigerator for at least 4 hours or overnight.

2   Heat the oil in a frying pan and fry the onion for 5 minutes. Add the garlic and mushrooms and cook for a further 2 minutes, stirring all the time. Stir in the herbs, mustard and a little of the stock.

3   Arrange the chicken quarters in a single layer (if possible) in the ceramic cooking pot. Pour over the marinade and the onion mixture. Add the rest of the stock and season with salt and pepper.

4   Cover with the lid and cook on Auto for 4–6 hours or on High for 3–4 hours or until the chicken is tender and thoroughly cooked.

5   Transfer the chicken to warmed plates. Stir the parsley into the sauce and adjust the seasoning if necessary. Ladle the sauce over the chicken.

6   Serve with new or sauté potatoes and a green vegetable.

Tip
• This dish is also good made with rosé or white wine instead of red. If liked, add a few whole baby carrots and baby new potatoes to the cooking pot to make an all-in-one dish.

chicken marengo

4

35 MINS

4-6 hrs AUTO

crusty bread

1.6 kg/3½ lb **whole chicken**

Salt and freshly ground black pepper

25 g/1 oz/2 tbsp **butter**

30 ml/2 tbsp **sunflower oil**

30 ml/2 tbsp **brandy**

1 **onion**, sliced

1 **garlic clove**, crushed or 5 ml/ 1 tsp garlic purée (paste)

30 ml/2 tbsp **plain (all-purpose) flour**

150 ml/¼ pint/⅔ cup **dry white wine**

1 x 400 g/14 oz/large **can of chopped tomatoes**

15 ml/1 tbsp **tomato purée (paste)**

100 g/4 oz **button mushrooms**, halved

A few slices of **pickled walnuts** or a handful of stoned (pitted) **black olives**

1   Cut the chicken into eight even-sized pieces and remove the skin. Season with salt and pepper.

2   Melt 15 ml/1 tbsp of the butter and 15 ml/1 tbsp of the oil in a frying pan and fry the chicken over a moderately hot heat for 3–4 minutes or until browned. Warm the brandy, pour over the pieces of chicken and ignite carefully by holding a match to the surface of the liquid. When the flames have subsided transfer to the ceramic cooking pot.

3   Add the remaining butter and oil to the pan and fry the onion and garlic for 4–5 minutes or until beginning to colour. Sprinkle over the flour and cook for 1 minute, stirring.

4   Gradually add the white wine, stirring all the time. Stir in the chopped tomatoes, tomato purée and mushrooms. Heat until steaming, but not boiling, then pour over the chicken.

5   Cover with the lid and cook on High or Auto for 1 hour. Turn to Low or leave on Auto and cook for a further 3–5 hours or until the chicken is very tender and cooked through. Stir in the pickled walnut slices or olives.

6   Serve with crusty bread.

Tip
• In this dish a whole chicken is cut into portions so that everyone can enjoy their favourite cut. You can of course use four chicken quarters or eight chicken thighs or drumsticks.

normandy chicken

4 | 30 MINS | 3-4 hrs HIGH | sauté potatoes and French (green) beans

Chef's note

Normandy is renowned for it fragrant apples and pears and rich dairy produce such as crème fraîche. These are combined to make this delicious chicken dish. This version is made with cider, but unsweetened apple juice makes a good alternative.

30 ml/2 tbsp **sunflower oil**

100 g/4 oz **smoked streaky bacon**, rind removed and cut into small pieces

1 bunch of **spring onions (scallions)**, trimmed and sliced

4 skinless **chicken supremes**, each about 150 g/5 oz

175 ml/6 fl oz/¾ cup **dry or medium apple or pear cider**

175 ml/6 fl oz/¾ cup hot **chicken stock**

5 ml/1 tsp chopped **fresh thyme** or 2.5 ml/½ tsp dried thyme

2 **firm pears**, peeled, quartered, cored and thickly sliced

Salt and freshly ground black pepper

60 ml/4 tbsp **crème fraîche**

1   Heat 10 ml/2 tsp of the oil in a non-stick frying pan, add the bacon and cook over a moderately high heat for 3 minutes. Add the spring onions and cook for a further minute, stirring until the bacon is browned. Transfer to the ceramic cooking pot with a slotted spoon, leaving all the fat behind in the pan.

2   Add the rest of the oil to the pan and fry the chicken until lightly browned on both sides. Add to the cooking pot and switch on the slow cooker to High.

3   Pour the cider into the pan and stir to remove any sediment. Pour over the chicken. Add the chicken stock, thyme, pears and salt and pepper.

4   Cover with the lid and cook for 3–4 hours or until the chicken is thoroughly cooked and tender. Transfer the chicken to warmed serving plates. Stir the crème fraîche into the sauce. Spoon the sauce over the chicken.

5   Serve with sauté potatoes and French beans.

Tip
• Chicken breasts still on the bone with the wing attached are known as chicken supremes and are superb in a casserole.

chicken rossini

4 | 40 MINS | 3-4 hrs LOW | croûtons or new potatoes and a green vegetable

Chef's note

In this recipe chicken breasts are flattened, rolled up with a pâté filling and cooked in a creamy mushroom sauce. The dish is traditionally garnished with croûtons; you can either buy these ready-made or make your own by frying cubes of white bread in hot oil for a few minutes until golden.

4 boneless **chicken breasts**, skinned

Salt and freshly ground black pepper

100 g/4 oz **firm pâté**, cut into 4 slices

25 g/1 oz/2 tbsp **butter**

10 ml/2 tsp **olive oil**

175 g/6 oz **button mushrooms**, thickly sliced

45 ml/3 tbsp **brandy**

150 ml/¼ pint/⅔ cup **chicken stock**

45 ml/3 tbsp **double (heavy) cream**

1   Put the chicken breasts between two sheets of oiled greaseproof (waxed) paper, baking parchment or clingfilm (plastic wrap) and gently hit with a rolling pin until about 1 cm/¾ in thick. Season with salt and pepper.

2   Wrap each slice of pâté in a flattened chicken breast and secure with wooden cocktail sticks (toothpicks). Melt 15 g/ ½ oz/1 tbsp of the butter and all the oil and fry the chicken until lightly browned, then transfer to the ceramic cooking pot.

3   Fry the mushrooms in the rest of the butter for 2 minutes, then add the brandy and stock and heat until steaming hot but not boiling. Season and pour over the chicken.

4   Cover with the lid and cook on Low for 3–4 hours or until the chicken is thoroughly cooked and tender.

5   Take the chicken breasts out of the casserole, remove the cocktail sticks and place on warmed plates. Stir the cream into the cooking juices and pour over the chicken.

6   Serve with croûtons or new potatoes and a green vegetable.

chicken chasseur

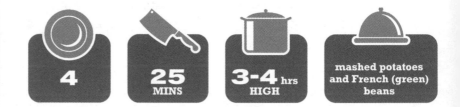

4

25 MINS

3-4 hrs HIGH

mashed potatoes and French (green) beans

Chef's note

This all-time classic is usually made with chicken breasts but in this simple version thighs have been used instead. The chicken is braised in a tomato and mushroom sauce with dry vermouth to make a healthy and hearty casserole.

1 **onion**, sliced

2 **garlic cloves**, crushed or 10 ml/2 tsp garlic purée (paste)

1 x 400 g/14 oz/large **can of chopped tomatoes**

150 ml/¼ pint/⅔ cup **dry vermouth**

100 g/4 oz **baby button mushrooms**

Salt and freshly ground black pepper

1 **bouquet garni sachet** or 5 ml/1 tsp dried mixed herbs

8 **chicken thighs**, skinned

1 Put the onion, garlic, tomatoes, vermouth and mushrooms in the ceramic cooking pot. Season generously with salt and pepper, then stir to mix.

2 Tuck the bouquet garni under the vegetables or stir in the dried mixed herbs, then place the chicken thighs on top, pushing them down gently to half-submerge in the liquid.

3 Cover with the lid and cook on High for 3–4 hours or until the chicken and vegetables are very tender. Remove the bouquet garni.

4 Serve with creamy mashed potatoes and steamed French beans.

Tips

- Make a bouquet garni by tying a bay leaf, a sprig of thyme and a couple of parsley stalks together with string, or if preferred place in a square of muslin (cheesecloth), tied at the top to make a bag.
- You could use dry white wine if you don't have vermouth.

chicken with juniper

Chef's note

This is a well-flavoured dish in which the chicken is marinated overnight in red wine, juniper berries and rosemary to give it extra flavour. You'll have to plan ahead for this recipe but it is well worth it.

4

30 MINS, plus marinating time

3-5 hrs HIGH

new potatoes

4 **chicken quarters**, skinned

3 **garlic cloves**, lightly crushed in their skin with the blade of a knife

7.5 ml/1½ tsp **juniper berries**, lightly crushed

2 **bay leaves**

2 sprigs of **fresh rosemary**, bruised

300 ml/½ pint/1¼ cups **red wine**

15 g/½ oz/4 tbsp **dried porcini mushrooms**

250 ml/8 fl oz/1 cup **boiling water**

12 **shallots**

30 ml/2 tbsp **olive oil**

45 ml/3 tbsp chopped **fresh or frozen parsley**

Salt and freshly ground black pepper

1   Place the chicken quarters in a snugly-fitting dish. Tuck the garlic, juniper, bay leaves and rosemary around the chicken, then pour the wine over. Cover tightly and marinate in the fridge for at least 4 hours or overnight.

2   Soak the mushrooms in boiling water for 10 minutes. Soak the shallots in enough boiling water to cover, for 5 minutes. Drain the shallots and peel off the skins when cool enough to handle. Cut each in half lengthways.

3   Remove the chicken from the marinade and pat dry. Heat the oil in a frying pan, add the chicken and cook for 3–4 minutes until lightly browned. Transfer to the ceramic cooking pot and switch on the slow cooker to High. Pour the marinade into the pan and heat gently until steaming hot but not boiling. Pour over the chicken.

4   Drain the mushrooms, adding most of the liquid to the slow cooker (leave the last spoonful or two as it may contain a little grit from the mushrooms). Chop the mushrooms and add them with the halved shallots.

5   Cover and cook for 3–5 hours or until the shallots and chicken are tender and thoroughly cooked. Discard the bay leaves and rosemary. Stir in the parsley and season to taste.

6   Serve with new potatoes.

hot southern chicken

4

25 MINS

2 hrs HIGH

complete meal in itself

Chef's note

This chicken recipe, spiced up with chilli and cooked with a selection of vegetables and rice, is a complete meal in itself. It can be ready in less than 2 hours so it's great to set up for a weekend lunch dish.

30 ml/2 tbsp **olive oil**

25 g/1 oz/2 tbsp **butter**

4 large skinless, boneless **chicken breasts**, each cut into 3 pieces

1 **large onion**, chopped

2 **garlic cloves**, finely chopped

1 **red chilli**, seeded and finely chopped

175 g/6 oz **okra (ladies' fingers)**

1 x 400 g/14 oz/large **can of chopped tomatoes**

400 ml/14 fl oz/1¾ cups hot **chicken stock**

175 g/6 oz/⅔ cup **easy-cook (converted) rice**

100 g/4 oz **canned or frozen sweetcorn**, thawed

Salt and freshly ground black pepper

1   Heat 15 ml/1 tbsp of the oil and 15 g/½ oz/1 tbsp of the butter in a frying pan, add the chicken and turn for 2–3 minutes until it is golden all over. Remove from the pan with a slotted spoon and place in the ceramic cooking pot. Switch on the slow cooker to High.

2   Add the remaining oil and butter to the pan. Add the onion, garlic and chilli and cook gently for 5–6 minutes, until softened. Stir in the okra and tomatoes.

3   Heat until steaming hot, but not boiling, then add to the slow cooker. Stir in the stock, cover with the lid and cook for 1 hour.

4   Stir in the rice and sweetcorn, then season with salt and pepper. Re-cover and cook for a further ¾–1 hour or until the chicken, vegetables and rice are tender and most of the liquid has been absorbed.

Tip

• If you enjoy really spicy food, sprinkle in a few drops of Tabasco sauce when adding the rice.

chicken in red pepper sauce

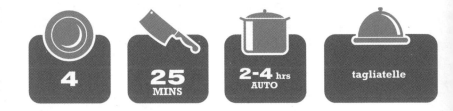

4

25 MINS

2-4 hrs AUTO

tagliatelle

Chef's note

In this low-fat chicken casserole, chicken breasts and red peppers are gently braised with white wine. The cooking juices are then puréed to make a stunning vibrant sauce.

1 **onion**, chopped

200 ml/7 fl oz/scant 1 cup hot **chicken stock**

2 **large red (bell) peppers**, seeded and roughly chopped

1 **garlic clove**, crushed or 5 ml/ 1 tsp garlic purée (paste)

120 ml/4 fl oz/½ cup **dry white wine** or orange juice

1 x 400 g/14 oz/1 large **can of chopped tomatoes**

Salt and freshly ground black pepper

1 **bay leaf**

4 skinless **chicken breast** fillets

1   Put the onion in the ceramic cooking pot. Pour over the stock, cover with the lid and switch on the slow cooker to Auto. Leave for a few minutes while preparing and measuring the remaining ingredients.

2   Stir the peppers into the onion mixture with the garlic, wine or orange juice, tomatoes, salt and pepper. Add the bay leaf, then place the chicken breasts on top.

3   Cover the cooking pot with the lid and cook on Auto for 2–4 hours or on Low for 3–4 hours until the chicken and vegetables are cooked through and tender.

4   Remove the chicken breasts from the cooking pot, cover and keep warm. Discard the bay leaf, then purée the sauce in a food processor or hand-held blender until smooth. Place the chicken breasts on warmed serving plates and pour over the sauce.

5   Serve at once with tagliatelle, garnished with chopped fresh herbs.

Tips

• Yellow (bell) peppers may be used instead of red ones for a change but avoid green peppers as they may become slightly discoloured and bitter after long slow cooking.
• Turkey breast steaks make an excellent alternative to chicken.

tomato & olive chicken

4   **20 MINS**   **2-3 hrs HIGH**   rice and a green vegetable

4 boneless, skinless **chicken breasts**, each about 150 g/5 oz

30 ml/2 tbsp **plain (all-purpose) flour**

Freshly ground black pepper

30 ml/2 tbsp **olive oil**

1 **bay leaf**

1 **garlic clove**, finely chopped

30 ml/2 tbsp **sun-dried tomato purée (paste)**

500 ml/17 fl oz/2¼ cups **chicken stock**

50 g/2 oz/⅓ cup stoned (pitted) **green olives**

1   Trim the chicken breasts and pat dry on kitchen paper (paper towels). Sprinkle with a light dusting of flour and pepper. Heat the oil in a frying pan, add the chicken and cook on both sides until lightly browned.

2   Transfer the chicken to the ceramic cooking pot and tuck the bay leaf underneath. Switch the slow cooker to High.

3   Blend together the garlic, sun-dried tomato purée and stock and pour over the chicken.

4   Cover with the lid and cook for 2–3 hours or until the chicken is tender. Add the olives about 30 minutes before the end of cooking time to allow them to heat through. Remove the bay leaf.

5   Serve with steamed or boiled rice and a green vegetable.

Tip

• Eight skinned, boneless chicken thighs may be used instead of chicken breasts.

chicken masala stew

Chef's note

Indian spices add warmth and colour to this delicious dish that is a cross between a stew and a soup. A steaming bowlful topped with a spoonful of thick, natural yoghurt and a sprinkling of chopped coriander is sure to please.

4

25 MINS

3-5 hrs LOW

chappatis or naan bread

1 **onion**, chopped

1 **garlic clove**, crushed or 5 ml/ 1 tsp garlic purée (paste)

5 ml/1 tsp **ground coriander**

5 ml/1 tsp **ground cumin**

2.5 ml/½ tsp **ground turmeric**

2.5 ml/½ tsp **ground ginger**

450 ml/¾ pint/2 cups hot **chicken stock**

400 g/14 oz **chicken breast** or **mini chicken fillets**

1 x 400 g/14 oz/large **can of chopped tomatoes**

200 g/7 oz **green beans**, halved

1 x 400 g/14 oz/large **can of chick peas (garbanzos)**, drained and rinsed

30 ml/2 tbsp **fresh or frozen chopped coriander (cilantro)**

Salt and freshly ground black pepper

1   Put the onion, garlic, ground coriander, cumin, turmeric and ginger in the ceramic cooking pot. Pour over the stock, cover with the lid and leave for a few minutes while measuring and preparing the remaining ingredients.

2   Cut the chicken into 2 cm/¾ in wide strips. Add to the cooking pot with the chopped tomatoes, beans and chick peas.

3   Stir well, then cover and cook for 3–5 hours on Low or until the chicken is tender and the vegetables are cooked.

4   Stir in the fresh or frozen coriander and season to taste with salt and pepper. Ladle into warmed bowls.

5   Serve straight away with chappatis or naan bread.

Tips

• To save time use 15 ml/1 tbsp of your favourite curry powder or paste instead of the individual dry spices.
• Extra vegetables may be added if liked, such as cubes of courgette (zucchini) or sweetcorn.

chicken gumbo

4

30 MINS

4-4½ hrs HIGH

rice

Chef's note

Okra is always added to gumbos – stews of meat, seafood or vegetables – from Louisiana and the southern United States of America. The seeds are surrounded by sticky juices that act as a thickening agent and give the sauce a smooth, silky finish.

15 g/½ oz/1 tbsp **unsalted (sweet) butter**

30 ml/2 tbsp **sunflower oil**

1.75 kg/4 lb **whole chicken**, cut into 8 pieces and skinned

1 **onion**, sliced

2 **garlic cloves**, crushed or 10 ml/ 2 tsp garlic purée (paste)

300 ml/½ pint/1¼ cups **chicken stock**

30 ml/2 tbsp **sun-dried tomato purée (paste)**

10 ml/2 tsp **Worcestershire sauce**

A pinch of **ground cloves**

A pinch of **dried chilli flakes** or hot chilli powder

Salt and freshly ground black pepper

225 g/8 oz **okra (ladies' fingers)**, trimmed and thinly sliced

1 **green (bell) pepper**, seeded and sliced

1   Heat the butter and 15 ml/1 tbsp of the oil in a large frying pan and brown the chicken on all sides. Remove with a slotted spoon, leaving any fat behind, and place in the ceramic cooking pot.

2   Add the rest of the oil to the pan and fry the onion for 6–7 minutes until almost soft. Stir in the garlic and cook for a few seconds.

3   Add the stock, tomato purée, Worcestershire sauce, cloves, chilli and salt and pepper. Stir until the tomato purée is well blended and heat until steaming hot. Pour over the chicken. Cover with the lid and cook on High for 3 hours.

4   Add the okra and green pepper to the casserole and cook for a further 1–1½ hours or until the chicken is cooked and tender and the sauce has thickened.

5   Serve with rice.

Tip
• Choose firm, small, bright green okra that snap cleanly and do not bend and avoid any that are browning at the tips or edges. To prepare, wash and carefully pare off the stalk without breaking the seed pod.

chicken parmigiana

4

25 MINS

3-4 hrs AUTO

tagliatelle

Chef's note

This simple Italian-style dish with whole chicken breasts slowly cooked in a chunky aubergine, mushroom and tomato sauce is sprinkled with Parmesan cheese and grilled before serving.

30 ml/2 tbsp **olive oil**

1 red onion, chopped

2 **garlic cloves**, crushed or 10 ml/2 tsp garlic purée (paste)

225 g/8 oz **mushrooms**, quartered

1 **large aubergine (eggplant)**, diced

450 g/1 lb **ripe plum tomatoes**, chopped

2.5 ml/½ tsp **dried mixed herbs**

4 skinless **chicken breasts**

Salt and freshly ground black pepper

45 ml/3 tbsp **Parmesan cheese**, freshly grated

1. Heat the oil in a frying pan, add the onion and cook for 3 minutes over a medium heat. Add the garlic and mushrooms and cook for a further 2–3 minutes, until lightly coloured, stirring often.

2. Tip the onion and mushrooms into the ceramic cooking pot, then add the diced aubergine, chopped tomatoes and herbs. Cover with the lid and cook on High or Auto for 1 hour.

3. Stir the mixture, then add the chicken breasts, completely submerging them in the vegetables. Season with salt and pepper. Re-cover and leave on Auto or turn down the temperature to Low. Cook for a further 2–3 hours or until the chicken is thoroughly cooked.

4. Transfer the chicken and vegetable mixture to a gratin dish (or leave in the ceramic cooking pot if it can be used under the grill (broiler)).

5. Sprinkle the top with Parmesan cheese and cook under a preheated moderate grill for about 2 minutes until the cheese is melted and lightly browned.

6. Serve straight away with tagliatelle.

Tip

• If liked, stir a 400 g/14 oz/large can of artichokes hearts, well drained and quartered, into the vegetable mixture when adding the chicken.

turkey & bean cassoulet

4

25 MINS

3-5 hrs AUTO

a green vegetable such as steamed, shredded cabbage

Chef's note

A warming combination of lean turkey, spicy sausage and beans makes this country dish from south-west France a hearty main meal. It is served, as is traditional, with a crisp breadcrumb topping.

1 **onion**, chopped

2 **garlic cloves**, crushed or 10 ml/2 tsp garlic purée (paste)

15 ml/1 tbsp **sun-dried tomato purée (paste)**

5 ml/1 tsp **dried thyme** or dried mixed herbs

300 ml/½ pint/1¼ cups hot **chicken or vegetable stock**

450 g/1 lb thickly cut **turkey steaks**

100 g/4 oz **coarse-cut dry-cured French sausage**, diced

2 x 400 g/14 oz/large **cans of mixed beans**, drained and rinsed

1 x 400 g/14 oz/large **can of chopped tomatoes**

30 ml/2 tbsp **olive oil**

100 g/4 oz/2 cups **fresh white breadcrumbs**

Salt and freshly ground black pepper

1   Put the onion in the ceramic cooking pot. Blend together the garlic, tomato purée, herbs and about half of the stock. Pour over the onion and switch on the slow cooker to Auto. Leave for a few minutes while measuring and preparing the remaining ingredients.

2   Cut the turkey steaks into strips about 2 cm/¾ in wide. Add to the cooking pot with the diced sausage and beans. Mix together the remaining stock and chopped tomatoes and pour into the cooking pot. Cover and cook for 3–5 hours or until the turkey and onions are very tender.

3   Towards the end of the cooking time, heat the oil in a frying pan until hot. Add the breadcrumbs and cook, stirring constantly, for 3–4 minutes or until lightly browned and crisp.

4   Season the turkey and bean mixture to taste with salt and pepper. Sprinkle over the browned breadcrumbs.

5   Serve straight away with a green vegetable such as steamed, shredded cabbage.

Tip

• Instead of the breadcrumb topping, make a garlic bread topping. Spoon the cassoulet into a heatproof casserole dish (Dutch oven). Cut 12 thin slices of French bread. Lightly butter them with 40 g/ 1½ oz/3 tbsp butter blended with 2 crushed garlic cloves or 10 ml/ 2 tsp garlic purée (paste). Arrange on top of the cassoulet and put under a moderately hot grill (broiler) for 3–5 minutes until lightly browned. Serve straight away.

thai turkey curry

4 | 5 MINS | 3-5 hrs LOW | rice or warmed naan bread

100 g/4 oz **creamed coconut**, roughly chopped

600 ml/1 pint/2½ cups hot **chicken or vegetable stock**

30 ml/2 tbsp **Thai green curry paste**

1 bunch of **spring onions (scallions)**, diagonally sliced

15 ml/1 tbsp **lemon juice**

400 g/14 oz thinly cut **turkey breast steaks**

400 g/14 oz **new potatoes**

200 g/7 oz **frozen peas**

Salt and freshly ground black pepper

45 ml/3 tbsp chopped **fresh or frozen coriander (cilantro)**

1   Put the creamed coconut into the ceramic cooking pot and pour over the stock. Stir until the coconut has dissolved, then stir in the curry paste, followed by the spring onions and lemon juice.

2   Cover with the lid and switch on the slow cooker to Low. Leave for a few minutes while measuring and preparing the rest of the ingredients.

3   Cut the turkey into thin strips and the potatoes into chunks. Add them to the slow cooker with the peas and season with salt and pepper. Cover and cook for 3–5 hours or until the chicken and vegetables are tender.

4   Taste and adjust the seasoning if necessary, then stir in the chopped coriander.

5   Serve with rice or warm naan bread.

Tips

- Thai green curry paste contains an array of spices including green chillies, lemon grass, galangal, coriander, cumin and tamarind.
- Strips of chicken, pork fillet or lean rump (sirloin) steak would make excellent alternatives to turkey.

turkey beanpot

4 | **25** MINS | **4-5** hrs LOW | rice or mashed potatoes and a green vegetable

Chef's note

Turkey thigh meat is very economical. Ask your butcher to remove the meat from the bone if you prefer.

30 ml/2 tbsp **sunflower oil**

700 g/1½ lb **turkey thigh meat**, cut into 2.5 cm/1 in cubes

1 **large onion**, sliced

1 **garlic clove**, crushed or 5 ml/ 1 tsp garlic purée (paste)

1 **red (bell) pepper**, seeded and chopped

15 ml/1 tbsp **plain (all-purpose) flour**

5 ml/1 tsp **ground ginger**

150 ml/¼ pint/⅔ cup **red wine**

15 ml/1 tbsp **Worcestershire sauce** or **soy sauce**

150 ml/¼ pint/⅔ cup hot **chicken stock**

1 x 400 g/14 oz/large **can of chopped tomatoes**

1 x 400 g/14 oz/large **can of mixed beans** or **butter (lima) beans**, drained and rinsed

2.5 ml/½ tsp **dried thyme**

Salt and freshly ground black pepper

1. Heat 15 ml/1 tbsp of the oil in a frying pan and fry the turkey over a moderately high heat for 2–3 minutes or until lightly browned all over. Lift out of the pan with a slotted spoon and transfer to the ceramic cooking pot.

2. Add the remaining oil to the frying pan and cook the onion for 6–7 minutes. Add the garlic and red pepper and cook for a further minute, then sprinkle over the flour and ginger. Cook for a few seconds, then turn down the heat and gradually stir in the wine. Let the mixture bubble for a minute.

3. Turn off the heat and stir in the Worcestershire or soy sauce. Pour the mixture over the turkey. Stir in the stock, tomatoes, beans and thyme, then season with salt and pepper.

4. Cover with a lid and cook on Low for 4–5 hours or until the turkey is cooked and tender.

5. Serve with rice or mashed potatoes and a green vegetable, if liked.

duck ragù

Slow cooking duck legs with wine make them beautifully tender and succulent. Here they are cooked in a casserole with baby new vegetables. This is the perfect dinner-party dish.

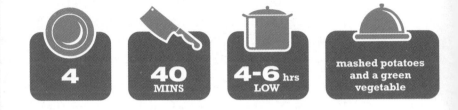

4

40 MINS

4-6 hrs LOW

mashed potatoes and a green vegetable

225 g/8 oz **button (pearl) onions** or **small shallots**, unpeeled

15 ml/1 tbsp **olive oil**

4 **duck legs**, about 200 g/7 oz each

225 g/8 oz **baby button mushrooms**

1 **garlic clove**, crushed or 5 ml/1 tsp garlic purée (paste)

2.5 ml/½ tsp **dried thyme**

1 **bay leaf**

30 ml/2 tbsp **cranberry jelly**

250 ml/8 fl oz/1 cup **red wine**

Salt and freshly ground black pepper

225 g/8 oz **baby carrots**

225 g/8 oz **baby turnips**, halved if large

600 ml/1 pint/2½ cups **chicken stock**

1 Put the onions or shallots in a heatproof bowl and pour over enough boiling water to cover. Leave for 5 minutes.

2 Meanwhile, heat the oil in a frying pan. Add the duck legs and cook for 5 minutes, turning until lightly browned on both sides. Transfer the duck to a plate.

3 Drain the onions and peel off the skins when cool enough to handle. Add to the frying pan and cook gently until they begin to brown. Add the mushrooms and garlic and cook for 2 minutes.

4 Stir in the thyme, bay leaf, cranberry jelly and wine. Let the mixture bubble for a minute, then turn off the heat. Season with salt and pepper.

5 Place a single layer of carrots and turnips in the ceramic cooking pot. Top with the duck legs, then arrange any remaining carrots and turnips around them. Pour over the onion and mushroom mixture. Pour in enough of the stock to just cover the duck and vegetables.

6 Cover with the lid and cook on Low for 4-6 hours or until the duck and vegetables are very tender. Remove the bay leaf.

7 Serve with creamy mashed potatoes and a green vegetable such as mangetout (snow peas).

chilli-braised duck with orange

 **4**

 **25** MINS, plus marinating time

 3-5 hrs LOW

 a green vegetable

Chef's note

Briefly marinating the duck breast lets all the flavours penetrate the meat. However, if you haven't time, don't worry; the duck will still be tender and delicious.

2 **oranges**

10 ml/2 tsp **sunflower oil**

A pinch of **dried chilli flakes**

4 skinless, boneless **duck breasts**, about 175 g/6 oz each

1 **onion**, very thinly sliced

4 **celery sticks**, sliced

400 g/14 oz **small new potatoes**, scrubbed (unpeeled) and halved

450 ml/¾ pint/2 cups hot **chicken or vegetable stock**

Salt and freshly ground black pepper

30 ml/2 tbsp chopped **fresh or frozen parsley**

1 Finely grate the zest from the oranges and squeeze out the juice. Whisk the zest and juice in a jug with the oil and chilli flakes.

2 Put the duck breasts in a dish in which they fit snugly, then pour over the orange juice mixture. Cover with clingfilm (plastic wrap) and marinate in the refrigerator for an hour, or overnight if preferred.

3 When you are ready to cook, remove the duck from the refrigerator and allow it to come to room temperature. Meanwhile, put the onion, celery, new potatoes and stock in the ceramic cooking pot and switch on to Low.

4 Put the duck on top of the vegetables. Season the marinade with a little salt and pepper and pour over. Cover with the lid and cook for 3–5 hours or until the duck and vegetables are tender.

5 Remove the duck from the slow cooker and leave on a board for a few minutes to rest, then cut into diagonal slices and arrange on warmed plates. Spoon the vegetables and sauce on to the plates and sprinkle with chopped parsley.

6 Serve with a green vegetable such as French beans or mangetout (snow peas).

Tip
• Buy unwaxed oranges if possible, as the skins will be free of preservatives.

fruity pheasant casserole

4

30 MINS

4-6 hrs HIGH

mashed root vegetables

30 ml/2 tbsp **sunflower oil**

4 boneless **pheasant breast fillets**, about 400 g/14 oz in total

1 **onion**, chopped

10 ml/2 tsp **plain (all-purpose) flour**

375 ml/13 fl oz/1½ cups **chicken stock**

2 **celery sticks**, sliced

2 **dessert (eating) apples**, peeled, cored and diced

Zest and juice of 1 **orange**

1 **bay leaf**

Salt and freshly ground black pepper

75 g/3 oz/¾ cup **chopped walnuts**

1   Heat the oil in a frying pan over a high heat. Add the pheasant fillets and briefly cook on both sides until lightly browned. Transfer to the ceramic cooking pot, leaving the fat and juices behind.

2   Add the onion to the pan and fry for 5–6 minutes until softened. Sprinkle over the flour and stir in, then gradually add the stock, stirring until bubbling and thickened. Turn off the heat.

3   Add the celery, apples, orange zest and juice and bay leaf to the cooking pot. Pour over the onions and stock. Season with salt and pepper. Cover with the lid and cook on High for 4–6 hours or until the pheasant and vegetables are tender and cooked. Remove the bay leaf.

4   Spoon on to warmed plates and serve scattered with the chopped walnuts.

5   Serve with mashed root vegetables, such as potatoes, carrots and swede (rutabaga).

Tip

• If liked, lightly toast the walnuts in a dry frying pan for a minute or two.

festive pheasant

| 4 | 30 MINS | 4-6 hrs AUTO | mashed potatoes and a green vegetable |

Chef's note

Serve with mashed potatoes and a green vegetable such as steamed, shredded cabbage

225 g/8 oz **button (pearl) onions**, unpeeled

4 boneless **pheasant breast fillets** or joints

Salt and freshly ground black pepper

25 g/1 oz/2 tbsp **unsalted (sweet) butter**

15 ml/1 tbsp **oil**

100 g/4 oz vacuum-packed peeled whole **chestnuts**

15 ml/1 tbsp **plain (all-purpose) flour**

150 ml/¼ pint/⅔ cup **dry white wine**

150 ml/¼ pint/⅔ cup **chicken stock**

15 ml/1 tbsp **redcurrant jelly (clear conserve)**

Finely grated zest and juice of 1 **orange**

30 ml/2 tbsp **brandy**

1 **bay leaf**

1 Put the onions in a heatproof bowl and pour over enough boiling water to cover. Leave for 5 minutes.

2 Sprinkle the pheasant with salt and pepper. Heat the butter and oil in a frying pan and fry the pheasant until browned all over. Transfer to the ceramic cooking pot, leaving the juices in the pan.

3 Drain the onions and peel off the skins when cool enough to handle. Add to the frying pan and cook for 2–3 minutes or until beginning to brown. Add to the pheasant with the chestnuts.

4 Sprinkle the flour over the fat remaining in the pan and cook over a low heat for a minute. Gradually add the wine and stock and bring to the boil, stirring. Stir in the redcurrant jelly, orange zest, juice and brandy. Turn off the heat.

5 Tuck the bay leaf under the pheasant, then pour over the wine and stock mixture. Cover and cook on High or Auto for 1 hour.

6 Leave on High or reduce the temperature to Auto and cook for a further 3–5 hours or until the pheasant and onions are tender and cooked. Remove the bay leaf.

7 Serve with creamy mashed potatoes and a green vegetable such as steamed, shredded cabbage.

Tips

- Pheasant breast fillets will take less time to cook than joints.
- You could use boneless chicken or turkey breast fillets instead of pheasant.

guinea fowl with red cabbage

4

30 MINS

3-4 hrs HIGH

crisp roast or sauté potatoes

Chef's note

Guinea fowl has a mildly gamey taste like a well-flavoured chicken and is delicious cooked on a bed of red cabbage braised with orange juice and plump sultanas.

25 g/1 oz/2 tbsp **unsalted (sweet) butter**, softened

450 g/1 lb **red cabbage**

15 ml/1 tbsp **sunflower oil**

1.5 kg/3 lb oven-ready **guinea fowl**, jointed

1 **small onion**, finely chopped

10 ml/2 tsp **plain (all-purpose) flour**

150 ml/¼ pint/⅔ cup **orange juice**

150 ml/¼ pint/⅔ cup hot **chicken stock**

30 ml/2 tbsp **sultanas (golden raisins)**

15 ml/1 tbsp **soft light brown sugar**

15 ml/1 tbsp **red wine vinegar**

4 **juniper berries**, lightly crushed

Salt and freshly ground black pepper

1. Grease the ceramic cooking pot with half the butter. Cut the cabbage into wedges and remove the central core from each, then shred as finely as possible. Put in the cooking pot, packing tightly.

2. Heat the remaining butter and the oil in a frying pan and brown the guinea fowl portions all over. Lift out of the pan, leaving the fat behind and place on top of the red cabbage.

3. Add the chopped onion to the pan and fry for 6–7 minutes until soft. Sprinkle over the flour and stir for a few seconds, then gradually add the orange juice, stirring.

4. Pour in the chicken stock and bring to the boil, stirring until bubbling and thickened. Turn off the heat. Stir in the sultanas, sugar, wine vinegar, juniper berries and salt and pepper. Pour the sauce over the guinea fowl.

5. Cover with a lid and cook on High for 3–4 hours or until the meat and cabbage are tender and thoroughly cooked.

6. Serve with roast or sauté potatoes.

Tip
- Chicken joints may be used instead of guinea fowl, if preferred.

marinated game casserole

4 | **30** MINS, plus marinating time | **5-6** hrs AUTO | game chips or celeriac (celery root) mash

For the marinade:

15 ml/1 tbsp **olive oil**

1 **onion**, chopped

2 **garlic cloves**, sliced

6 **allspice berries**, lightly crushed

6 **black peppercorns**, lightly crushed

30 ml/2 tbsp **red wine vinegar**

60 ml/4 tbsp **redcurrant jelly (clear conserve)**

2 **bay leaves**

For the casserole:

4 **pigeons (squabs)**, each about 225 g/8 oz

30 ml/2 tbsp **olive oil**

1 **onion**, chopped

225 g/8 oz **mushrooms**, sliced

15 ml/1 tbsp **plain (all-purpose) flour**

250 ml/8 fl oz/1 cup **chicken or vegetable stock**

Salt and freshly ground black pepper

30 ml/2 tbsp chopped **fresh parsley**

1   Mix all the ingredients for the marinade in a large dish in which the pigeons will fit snugly. Add the pigeons, submerging in the marinade, then cover and chill for 8 hours, or overnight if preferred.

2   Heat the oil in a frying pan and fry the onion for 3 minutes. Add the mushrooms and cook for a further 3–4 minutes or until beginning to soften.

3   Sprinkle over the flour and cook for a few seconds, then gradually add the stock. Bring to the boil, stirring until slightly thickened, then turn off the heat. Season with salt and pepper.

4   Remove the pigeons from the marinade and place them in the ceramic cooking pot. Pour over the thickened stock mixture, then strain in the marinade through a sieve (strainer), discarding the spices and other flavouring ingredients.

5   Cover and cook on High or Auto for 1 hour, then leave on Auto or reduce the temperature to Low and cook for a further 4–5 hours or until the pigeons are thoroughly cooked and tender.

6   Serve with game chips or celeriac mash, garnished with chopped fresh parsley.

Tip

• Game chips are extra-large, chunky chips. You can buy them frozen and simply oven bake them according to the packet instructions, or cut thick, large chips, leaving on the skins, parboil for 4 minutes, then drain well and deep-fry.

venison & cranberry stew

4

25 MINS

4-6 hrs LOW

mashed potatoes and Savoy cabbage

450 g/1 lb boneless **casserole venison**

250 ml/8 fl oz/1 cup **red wine**

60 ml/4 tbsp **cranberry sauce**

2 **garlic cloves**, crushed or 10 ml/2 tsp garlic purée (paste)

5 ml/1 tsp **dried thyme** or mixed herbs

1 **onion**, chopped

250 ml/8 fl oz/1 cup hot **beef stock**

2 **back (Canadian) bacon** rashers (slices)

4 **carrots**, halved lengthways and cut into 2.5 cm/1 in chunks

Salt and freshly ground black pepper

1   Cut the venison into 4 cm/1½ in cubes. Place in a bowl and pour over the wine. Add the cranberry sauce, garlic, dried thyme or mixed herbs and leave to marinate for a few minutes while measuring and preparing the rest of the ingredients.

2   Put the onion in the ceramic cooking pot. Pour in the stock, cover with the lid and switch on the slow cooker to Low.

3   Cut the rind and fat off the bacon, then snip the bacon into small pieces with kitchen scissors. Add to the ceramic cooking pot with the venison and marinade and the carrots. Season with salt and pepper.

4   Cover and cook for 4–6 hours or until the meat is very tender and the vegetables are cooked.

5   Serve with creamy mashed potatoes and Savoy cabbage or another green vegetable.

Tips

- Beef stewing steak (braising beef) may be used instead of venison if you prefer and redcurrant rather than cranberry sauce.
- Marinate at room temperature for 30 minutes before cooking if time allows (or for up to 12 hours in the refrigerator). This allows the flavours to penetrate the meat and tenderises it.

Healthy and **delicious**, fish is eminently suitable for the slow cooker as the **gentle**, even cooking ensures that it retains its **shape** and **texture** and doesn't disintegrate during cooking.

Although large whole fish won't fit in the slow cooker, it's absolutely perfect for fish steaks and fillets. Unlike meat, fish cooks relatively quickly in the slow cooker so is unsuitable for all-day cooking and many of the dishes in this chapter, such as Smoky Seafood Stew (see page 198) and Seafood Chowder (see page 220), cook in less than 2 hours.

Fish is a great source of protein and provides many vitamins and minerals. White fish is particularly low in fat making it the perfect food for helping to maintain a healthy weight. Try Fish Provençal (see page 194). Ideally, you should eat oily fish, such as salmon and fresh tuna, once a week as it contains beneficial heart-healthy fats. Dishes such as Coconut Salmon Casserole (see page 200) or Fresh Tuna Casserole (see page 212) make healthy and convenient meals.

When buying fish, remember that if it's really fresh it shouldn't smell 'fishy'. Obviously it's difficult to test pre-packed fish for freshness but buy from a reliable source and make sure that it looks firm and moist. Both fresh and frozen seafood should be put in the refrigerator or freezer as soon as possible and, ideally, fresh fish should be cooked and eaten on the day you buy it.

fish provençal

Chef's note

This colourful dish contains the classic combination of tomatoes, onions, olives and peppers to give a distinct Mediterranean flavour. You can use any firm-fleshed white fish: cod, haddock, coley, for example.

4

25 MINS

1 ¾ hrs AUTO

French bread and salad or new potatoes and green beans

30 ml/2 tbsp **olive oil**

2 **red onions**, sliced

2 **courgettes (zucchini)**, sliced

1 **red (bell) pepper**, seeded and sliced

1 **yellow (bell) pepper**, seeded and sliced

450 g/1 lb **ripe tomatoes**, skinned and roughly chopped

175 ml/6 fl oz/¾ cup **medium-dry white wine**

175 ml/6 fl oz/¾ cup hot **vegetable stock**

2.5 ml/½ tsp **dried Mediterranean** or **dried mixed herbs**

4 x 150 g/5 oz firm **white fish fillets**

Freshly ground black pepper

12 stoned (pitted) **black olives**

15 ml/1 tbsp **capers in brine**, drained

1 Heat the oil in a frying pan, add the onion and fry gently for 5 minutes. Add the courgettes and sliced peppers and cook for a further 2–3 minutes until almost softened.

2 Transfer to the ceramic cooking pot and stir in the tomatoes, wine, stock and herbs. Cover with the lid and switch on the slow cooker to Auto or High. Cook for 1 hour.

3 Meanwhile, skin the fish if necessary and cut the flesh into bite-sized pieces. Season with a little black pepper. Stir the fish pieces into the vegetables and reduce the temperature to Low or leave on Auto. Cook for 30 minutes or until the fish is almost cooked and the vegetables nearly tender.

4 Stir in the olives and capers. Re-cover and cook for a final 10–15 minutes to allow the fish and vegetables to finish cooking and the olives and capers to heat through.

5 Serve with French bread and salad or new potatoes and green beans.

Tip
- To skin tomatoes, place them in a heatproof bowl and pour over enough boiling water to cover. Leave for 1 minute, then drain and briefly rinse under cold water. The skins should now peel off easily.

classic bouillabaisse

Chef's note

Bouillabaisse is made with many different types of fish and shellfish and has a rich, flavoursome stock made from fish trimmings and prawn shells; the slow cooker is absolutely perfect for making this.

4 | **45** MINS | **2** hrs AUTO + **1** hr HIGH | crusty French bread and rouille

1 **onion**, sliced

2 **carrots**, finely sliced

6 **white peppercorns**

1 sprig of **fresh thyme**

1 **bay leaf**

A pinch of **saffron strands**

Strip of pared **orange zest**

350 g/12 oz raw unpeeled **tiger prawns (shrimp)**

900 g/2 lb **fish bones and trimmings**

150 ml/¼ pint/⅔ cup **white wine**

600 ml/1 pint/2½ cups **water**

450 g/1 lb firm **white fish fillets**, cut into large chunks

350 g/12 oz shell-on **mussels**, scrubbed and bearded

45 ml/3 tbsp chopped **fresh parsley**

1   Arrange the onion and carrots in the base of the ceramic cooking pot. Sprinkle over the peppercorns, then add the thyme, bay leaf, saffron and orange zest.

2   Remove the shells from the prawns and place the shells in the ceramic cooking pot. De-vein the prawns if necessary, then put in a bowl, cover and leave in the fridge until needed.

3   Rinse the bones and trimmings well under cold water and cut any larger pieces into chunks. Place in the pot and pour over the wine and water.

4   Cover and cook on High or Auto for 1 hour. Skim off any surface scum. Reduce the temperature to Low, re-cover and cook for 1 hour (no longer than this or the stock may become bitter). Turn off the slow cooker.

5   Strain the stock, then return it to the rinsed-out ceramic cooking pot. Switch on to High and heat for 30 minutes or until steaming hot. Meanwhile, remove the prawns from the fridge.

6   Add the fish chunks, prawns and mussels (discard any open ones). Cover and cook for a further 20–30 minutes or until the mussels have opened and the prawns are pink. Discard any mussels that have not opened. Sprinkle with the parsley.

7   Serve straight away with plenty of crusty French bread and a spoonful of rouille, if liked.

smoky seafood stew

4 | **25** MINS | **1** hr LOW | mashed potatoes and peas

Chef's note

This is a simple dish with minimal preparation. Don't worry if the sauce seems a little thick when you pour it over the raw fish and prawns; the juices from the seafood will dilute it as it cooks.

450 g/1 lb **smoked haddock fillet**, skinned

100 g/4 oz **raw shelled prawns (shrimp)**

1 **bay leaf**

25 g/1 oz/¼ cup **plain (all-purpose) flour**

25 g/1 oz/2 tbsp **butter**

300 ml/½ pint/1¼ cups **milk**

5 ml/1 tsp **made English mustard**

15 ml/1 tbsp **lemon juice**

60 ml/4 tbsp **soured (dairy sour) cream** or **crème fraîche**

1 x 200 g/7 oz/small **can of sweetcorn with added peppers**

Salt and freshly ground black pepper

30 ml/2 tbsp chopped **fresh or frozen parsley** (optional)

1 Cut the haddock into about 2.5 cm/1 in chunks. Put in the ceramic cooking pot with the prawns and bay leaf.

2 Put the flour, butter and milk in a saucepan. Place over a medium heat and stir all the time until the mixture thickens and bubbles.

3 Turn off the heat and stir the mustard, lemon juice, soured cream and sweetcorn into the sauce. Season with a little salt and pepper (don't add too much salt as the fish will already be slightly salty).

4 Pour the sauce over the fish and prawns and stir well to mix. Cover with the lid and cook on Low for 1 hour or until the fish is cooked and the prawns are pink.

5 Remove the bay leaf. Stir in the parsley, if using, then taste and adjust the seasoning if necessary.

6 Serve with creamy mashed potatoes and peas.

Tips

- If liked, replace half the milk with fish or vegetable stock and use 5 ml/1 tsp anchovy essence instead of the mustard.
- Try to buy natural smoked haddock rather than the bright-yellow, dyed variety as it has a better flavour.

coconut salmon casserole

4

20 MINS

1 hr HIGH

basmati rice or naan bread

Chef's note

With its creamy and mildly spiced coconut sauce, this dish makes a wonderful change from plain poached or grilled fish.

15 ml/1 tbsp **sunflower oil**

3 **shallots**, roughly chopped

1 **red chilli**, seeded and roughly chopped

1 **garlic clove**, crushed or 5 ml/ 1 tsp garlic purée (paste)

2.5 cm/1 in piece of **fresh root ginger**, peeled and grated

5 ml/1 tsp **ground cumin**

5 ml/1 tsp **ground coriander**

2.5 ml/½ tsp **ground turmeric**

100 g/4 oz **creamed coconut**, roughly chopped

450 ml/¾ pint/2 cups hot **vegetable stock**

4 x 150 g/5 oz **salmon steaks**, skins removed

Salt and freshly ground black pepper

1   Heat the oil in a frying pan and gently fry the shallots for 5 minutes. Add the chilli, garlic and ginger and cook for 2–3 minutes or until the shallots are soft.

2   Add the cumin, coriander and turmeric and cook for about 30 seconds, stirring all the time. Turn off the heat and stir in the coconut and about half of the stock. Stir until the coconut has dissolved.

3   Pour the mixture into a blender or food processor and purée until smooth. Add the rest of the stock and briefly blend again.

4   Pour about half of the sauce into the ceramic cooking pot and switch on the slow cooker to High. Season the salmon steaks with salt and pepper and add to the cooking pot.

5   Pour the rest of the sauce over, cover with the lid and cook for 1 hour on High or until the salmon is just cooked.

6   Carefully remove the salmon from the slow cooker and place on warmed plates with the sauce spooned over.

7   Accompany with steamed or boiled basmati rice or warm naan bread.

fish nuggets in tomato sauce

4

30 MINS

1³⁄₄-2 hrs LOW

rice or noodles

Chef's note

Providing you buy really fresh fish, these tasty nuggets can be made up to a day in advance and chilled until you are ready to cook them. Use any firm white fish; an inexpensive tail piece would be ideal.

1 x 400 g/14 oz/large **can of chopped tomatoes**

150 ml/¼ pint/⅔ cup **vegetable stock**

100 ml/3½ fl oz/scant ½ cup **white wine** or extra stock

150 g/5 oz **button mushrooms**, very finely sliced

2.5 ml/½ tsp **dried mixed herbs**

400 g/1 lb skinned and boned **white fish**

50 g/2 oz/1 cup **fresh white breadcrumbs**

6 **spring onions (scallions)**, finely chopped

Salt and freshly ground black pepper

1   Put the tomatoes, stock, wine or extra stock, mushrooms and herbs in the ceramic cooking pot and switch on the slow cooker to High. Cover with the lid and cook for 1 hour.

2   Meanwhile, roughly chop the fish and put it in a food processor with the breadcrumbs and spring onions. Season generously with salt and pepper and process until the fish is finely chopped but not completely smooth.

3   With dampened hands, shape the fish mixture into 20 even-sized balls. Chill in the refrigerator until ready to cook.

4   Add the fish nuggets to the sauce and cook for a further 45 minutes–1 hour or until they are thoroughly cooked and the mushrooms are tender.

5   Serve with boiled or steamed rice or noodles.

Tip
• Four thinly sliced baby courgettes (zucchini) can be used instead of the mushrooms, if preferred.

red mullet & fennel casserole

| 4 | 25 MINS | 2¾ hrs HIGH | rice or couscous |

Chef's note

This is a great way to cook fish fillets. Red mullet is a Mediterranean fish and is at its best during the summer months. It is often cooked whole but will fit better in the slow cooker if filleted.

2 **fennel bulbs**

30 ml/2 tbsp **olive oil**

400 ml/14 fl oz/1¾ cups hot **vegetable stock**

8 **ripe tomatoes**

2 sprigs of **fresh rosemary**

15 ml/1 tbsp **balsamic vinegar**

2 **garlic cloves**, crushed or 10 ml/2 tsp garlic purée (paste)

Salt and freshly ground black pepper

4 large **red mullet**, filleted but unskinned

1   Trim the fennel bulbs, then cut into thin slices from the top to the root end. Heat 15 ml/1 tbsp of the oil in a frying pan and cook the slices over a medium heat for 8–10 minutes, turning once, until almost tender and very lightly browned on both sides.

2   Transfer to the ceramic cooking pot and pour the stock over. Cover with the lid and switch on the slow cooker to High for a few minutes while preparing the tomatoes.

3   Place the tomatoes in a heatproof bowl and cover with boiling water. Leave for 1 minute, drain and briefly run under cold water. Peel off the skins. Quarter and seed the tomatoes, then cut into small pieces. Scatter the tomatoes over the fennel, top with the rosemary, then re-cover and cook for 2 hours.

4   Mix together the remaining oil, balsamic vinegar, garlic and salt and pepper and lightly brush over the mullet fillets. Place skin-side down on top of the fennel mixture and cook for 45 minutes or until the fish is just cooked. Discard the rosemary.

5   Serve with rice or couscous.

Tip
- The distinctive flavour of fennel goes well with other oily fish such as mackerel and trout. It would also work with white fish fillets, such as plaice, dotted with a little herby butter instead of the garlicky oil and vinegar mixture.

mediterranean braised turbot

4 **20 MINS** **1 ½ hrs LOW** **French bread**

Chef's note

In this recipe turbot is simply cooked with fragrant orange and herbs and a glassful of white wine for a trouble-free way to cook fish. It is low in fat too.

1 bunch of **spring onions (scallions)**, trimmed and thinly sliced

2 **garlic cloves**, crushed or 10 ml/2 tsp garlic purée (paste)

1 sprig of **fresh thyme** or 2.5 ml/½ tsp dried thyme

1 **bay leaf**

2 thinly pared strips of **orange zest**

120 ml/4 fl oz/½ cup **white wine**

4 x 150 g/5 oz pieces of **turbot fillet**, skinned

Salt and freshly ground black pepper

Juice of 1 **orange**

120 ml/4 fl oz/½ cup **vegetable stock**

4 **tomatoes**, sliced

A handful of stoned (pitted) **black olives**

1   Put the spring onions, garlic, thyme, bay leaf and orange zest in the ceramic cooking pot. Pour over the wine, cover with the lid and switch on the slow cooker to Low.

2   Lightly season the fish with salt and pepper, then place on top of the onion and herb mixture.

3   Drizzle the orange juice over the fish, then arrange the tomato slices on top. Scatter the olives around the sides and pour in the stock.

4   Cover with the lid and cook for 1¼–1½ hours on Low or until the fish is opaque and flakes easily.

5   Transfer the fish to warmed plates. Discard the thyme sprig, bay leaf and orange zest and spoon the sauce over the fish.

6   Serve with warm, crusty French bread.

Tip
• Don't worry if the fish isn't completely submerged in the liquid. It cooks through a combination of braising and steaming.

haddock casserole

4

20 MINS

1-2 hrs LOW

creamy mashed potatoes

700 g/1½ lb **haddock or other white fish**, skinned and cubed

15 ml/1 tbsp **cornflour (cornstarch)**

15 ml/1 tbsp **sunflower oil**

1 **onion**, finely chopped

1 **garlic clove**, crushed or 5 ml/1 tsp garlic purée (paste)

225 g/8 oz **courgettes (zucchini)**, thinly sliced

150 ml/¼ pint/⅔ cup **dry white wine** or **cider**

150 ml/¼ pint/⅔ cup **fish or vegetable stock**

1 **bouquet garni sachet**

Salt and freshly ground black pepper

1 Toss the fish in the cornflour until well coated, shaking off any excess.

2 Heat the oil in a frying pan and fry the onion, garlic and courgettes for 6–7 minutes until fairly soft and just beginning to colour. Turn off the heat and stir in the wine or cider. Tip into the ceramic cooking pot.

3 Pour in the stock, then add the fish and bouquet garni. Season with salt and pepper. Stir well and cover with the lid.

4 Cook on Low for 1–2 hours or until the fish and vegetables are cooked. Discard the bouquet garni.

5 Serve with creamy mashed potatoes.

saffron seafood casserole

4

25 MINS

1 ½ hrs LOW

a green vegetable

50 g/2 oz/¼ cup **butter**

1 **garlic clove**, crushed or 5 ml/ 1 tsp garlic purée (paste)

1 **onion**, chopped

1 **leek**, thinly sliced

450 g/1 lb **haddock fillet**, skinned and cubed

450 g/1 lb **small new potatoes**, quartered

A pinch of **saffron strands**

150 ml/¼ pint/⅔ cup hot **fish or vegetable stock**

150 ml/¼ pint/⅔ cup **white wine**

Salt and freshly ground black pepper

175 g/6 oz **mixed cooked seafood**

150 ml/¼ pint/⅔ cup **single (light) cream**

15 ml/1 tbsp chopped **fresh tarragon**

Chef's note

A fish casserole can be transformed by the addition of fragrant saffron, which gives the sauce a vibrant golden colour. It's very expensive, so only use a small pinch.

1   Melt the butter in a frying pan and gently fry the garlic, onion and leek for 6–7 minutes until soft. Tip into the ceramic cooking pot.

2   Add the haddock, new potatoes, saffron, stock and wine. Season with a little salt and pepper and gently stir together.

3   Cover and cook on Low for 1 hour or until the fish and potatoes are almost cooked.

4   Stir in the seafood, cream and tarragon. Cook for a further 30 minutes or until the fish and potatoes are cooked through and the seafood is hot.

5   Serve with a green vegetable, such as French beans.

Tip

• You'll find mixed seafood at the fish counter or in the frozen fish section. The contents may vary but will usually be a combination of prawns (shrimp), mussels and squid. If you prefer, prawns alone may be used. Thoroughly defrost and drain if frozen.

fresh tuna casserole

4 **25 MINS** **10 mins HIGH + 8 hrs LOW** **French (green) beans**

Chef's note

Onions will caramelise to a rich golden colour if cooked slowly for a long time. A dash of balsamic vinegar enhances them and gives a wonderful sweet and sour flavour. The tuna steaks are added towards the end of cooking.

50 g/2 oz/¼ cup **unsalted (sweet) butter**

30 ml/2 tbsp **olive oil**

4 **onions**, thinly sliced

10 ml/2 tsp **caster (superfine) sugar**

1 **red (bell) pepper**, seeded and thinly sliced

1 **yellow (bell) pepper**, seeded and thinly sliced

30 ml/2 tbsp **balsamic vinegar**

2.5 ml/½ tsp **dried thyme**

4 x 150 g/5 oz **tuna loin steaks**

Salt and freshly ground black pepper

5 ml/1 tsp **cornflour (cornstarch)**

15 ml/1 tbsp **water**

150 ml/¼ pint/⅔ cup **vegetable stock** or **a mixture of white wine and stock**

1   Put the butter and 15 ml/1 tbsp of the oil in the ceramic cooking pot and heat on High for about 10 minutes until the butter has melted.

2   Add the onions and stir well to coat in the melted mixture. Cover with the lid, then place a folded tea towel (dish cloth) over the top to retain the heat. Turn the heat down to Low and cook for 3 hours, stirring every hour.

3   Sprinkle the sugar over the onions and stir well. Replace the lid and the tea towel and cook for a further 2 hours, stirring once.

4   Stir in the red and yellow peppers, vinegar and thyme. Cook for 2 hours, stirring half way through cooking. By this time the onions should be golden and the pepper slices tender.

5   Lightly brush the tuna on both sides with the remaining oil and season with salt and pepper. Blend the cornflour with the water, then mix with the stock or wine and stock mixture. Pour into the cooking pot, stir well, then place the tuna on top of the vegetables.

6   Cover again and cook for ¾–1 hour or until the fish is tender and cooked through.

7   Serve with French beans, or another green vegetable.

Tip
• Other firm fish such as swordfish, cod loin or sea bass can be cooked in this way.

fresh swordfish with lentils

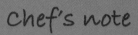
Chef's note

Puy lentils are dark green in colour and have a unique peppery flavour. They retain their shape even after long, slow cooking, which makes them perfect for this dish. This can be a complete meal in itself, but you may like to serve it with some crusty French bread.

4 **25 MINS** **3½ hrs HIGH** **crusty French bread**

---

30 ml/2 tbsp **olive oil**

3 **red onions**, each cut into 8 wedges

2 **fennel bulbs**, thinly sliced

2 **garlic cloves**, crushed or 10 ml/2 tsp garlic purée (paste)

1 **red chilli**, seeded and finely chopped

2.5 ml/½ tsp **dried mixed herbs**

200 g/7 oz/1¼ cups **Puy lentils**, rinsed

900 ml/1½ pints/3¾ cups hot **vegetable stock**

4 x 150 g/5 oz **swordfish steaks**

Salt and freshly ground black pepper

1   Heat 15 ml/1 tbsp of the oil in a frying pan, add the onions and fennel and cook gently for 7–8 minutes until almost soft. Stir in the garlic, chilli and herbs and cook for a further minute.

2   Transfer the mixture to the ceramic cooking pot, stir in the lentils and stock and cover with the lid. Turn on the slow cooker to High and cook for 2½ hours or until the lentils are just tender.

3   Brush both sides of the swordfish steaks with the remaining oil. Season the lentil mixture with salt and pepper and stir.

4   Place the swordfish on top of the lentils, re-cover and cook for ¾–1 hour or until the fish and lentils are cooked.

5   Serve with crusty French bread, if liked.

Tip

- Take care when preparing chillies. Wash your hands well afterwards as the juices can cause burning irritation, especially if you touch your eyes or lips. If you enjoy spicy food buy a jar of ready-chopped chillies; once opened, this will keep in the refrigerator for a couple of months. A large pinch of dried chilli flakes may be used instead.

malay-style fish casserole

4

25 MINS

1 ½ hrs HIGH

white basmati or jasmine rice

Chef's note

You can use any firm white fish for this recipe but it does work well with monkfish.

15 ml/1 tbsp **sunflower oil**

6 **spring onions (scallions)**, chopped

1 **garlic clove**, crushed or 5 ml/ 1 tsp garlic purée (paste)

1 **red chilli**, seeded and thinly sliced

1 **red (bell) pepper**, seeded and sliced

10 ml/2 tsp **ground coriander**

5 ml/1 tsp **ground cumin**

2.5 ml/½ tsp **ground turmeric**

1 x 200 g/7 oz/small **can of chopped tomatoes**

250 ml/8 fl oz/1 cup hot **fish or vegetable stock**

150 ml/¼ pint/⅔ cup **coconut milk**

30 ml/2 tbsp **nam pla fish sauce** or light soy sauce

1 x 200 g/7 oz/small **can of bamboo shoots**, drained

550 g/1¼ lb thick **white fish fillet**

12 raw **tiger prawns (shrimp)**

15 ml/1 tbsp **lime or lemon juice**

30 ml/2 tbsp chopped fresh or frozen **coriander (cilantro)**

Salt and freshly ground black pepper

1   Heat the oil in a frying pan. Add the spring onions, garlic, chilli and red pepper and cook for 3 minutes, until beginning to soften. Stir in the coriander, cumin and turmeric and cook for a few more seconds, then turn off the heat.

2   Stir in the chopped tomatoes, then tip the mixture into the ceramic cooking pot. Stir in the stock, coconut milk, fish sauce or light soy sauce and bamboo shoots. Stir well.

3   Cover with the lid and switch on the slow cooker to High. Cook for 45 minutes.

4   Skin the fish fillets and remove any bones. Cut into bite-sized chunks. Peel and devein the tiger prawns. Add the fish and prawns to the cooking pot and cook for 45 minutes or until the fish is cooked and the prawns are pink.

5   Stir in the lime or lemon juice and coriander. Taste and add salt and pepper if necessary.

6   Serve with boiled or steamed white basmati or jasmine rice.

fish in spicy tomato sauce

4

20 MINS

1 ¾-2 hrs AUTO

warmed pitta bread or matzos; rice or noodles

Chef's note

This is a simple version of the traditional Jewish fish casserole known as Samak. The rich sauce goes well with chunky white fish such as cod or haddock.

15 ml/1 tbsp **sunflower oil**

1 **onion**, finely chopped

1 **garlic clove**, crushed, or 5 ml/ 1 tsp garlic purée (paste)

1 **red chilli**, seeded and finely chopped

5 ml/1 tsp **curry powder or paste**

1.5 ml/¼ tsp **ground turmeric**

1.5 ml/¼ tsp **ground ginger**

150 ml/¼ pint/⅔ cup **passata (sieved tomatoes)**

100 ml/3½ fl oz/scant ½ cup **fish or vegetable stock**

5 ml/1 tsp **caster (superfine) sugar**

15 ml/1 tbsp fresh or bottled **lemon juice**

Salt and freshly ground black pepper

750 g/1¾ lb firm **white fish fillets**, skinned

30 ml/2 tbsp chopped **fresh parsley** or **coriander (cilantro)**

1 Heat the oil in a frying pan and cook the onion for 5–6 minutes until beginning to soften. Stir in the garlic, chilli, curry powder or paste, turmeric and ginger. Cook for 1 minute, stirring all the time. Turn off the heat.

2 Stir in the passata, stock, sugar and lemon juice. Season with salt and pepper, then tip the mixture into the ceramic cooking pot. Cover with the lid and cook on Auto or High for 1 hour.

3 Add the fish to the cooking pot, arranging in a single layer and submerging in the sauce. Re-cover and cook on Auto or turn down the temperature to Low for 45 minutes–1 hour or until the fish is tender and just cooked through.

4 Lift the fish on to warmed serving plates. Stir the parsley or coriander into the sauce. Taste the sauce and add a little more lemon juice if needed. Spoon the sauce over the fish.

5 Serve straight away with warmed pitta bread or matzos, or with rice or noodles, if you prefer.

seafood chowder

4 | **25 MINS** | **1 ¾ hrs HIGH** | crusty French bread

Chef's note

The name 'chowder' comes from the French word chaudière, the name of the pot that was traditionally used for making soups and casseroles. This recipe is a cross between these two dishes and is a tasty mixture of fresh seafood and rice flavoured with smoky bacon.

25 g/1 oz/2 tbsp **unsalted (sweet) butter**

2 rindless **smoked streaky bacon** rashers (slices), chopped

1 **leek**, finely sliced

1 **garlic clove**, crushed or 5 ml/1 tsp garlic purée (paste)

10 ml/2 tsp **plain (all-purpose) flour**

450 ml/¾ pint/2 cups **vegetable stock**

175 g/6 oz/1½ cup **sweetcorn**, drained if canned or defrosted if frozen

375 ml/13 fl oz/1½ cups **milk**

Salt and freshly ground black pepper

100 g/4 oz/½ cup **easy-cook (converted) rice**

4 shelled **scallops**

175 g/6 oz firm **white fish fillet**

30 ml/2 tbsp chopped **fresh parsley**

30 ml/2 tbsp **single (light) cream** (optional)

1   Melt the butter in a frying pan. Add the bacon and leek and cook over a moderate heat, stirring frequently, for 7–8 minutes or until the leeks are soft but not browned. Stir in the garlic and cook for a further minute.

2   Sprinkle over the flour and stir in, then gradually add about half of the stock. Bring to the boil, stirring until thickened. Turn off the heat and leave to cool for a few minutes before tipping into the ceramic cooking pot.

3   Meanwhile, put the sweetcorn in a blender or food processor with the rest of the stock and blend until fairly smooth. Add to the cooking pot with the milk, salt and pepper, then cover with the lid and cook on High for 1 hour.

4   Add the rice to the pot and stir to combine, then re-cover and cook for 30 minutes. Meanwhile, pull the corals away from the scallops and cut the fish into bite-sized chunks.

5   Add the scallops (but not the corals) and fish to the chowder and gently stir. Cover and cook for 15 minutes.

6   Stir the corals and parsley into the chowder and cook for a further 5 minutes or until the vegetables, seafood and rice are cooked. Stir in the cream.

7   Serve with crusty French bread.

Tip
• You can use any firm-fleshed white fish for this recipe, from cod to monkfish.

vegetables & pulses

You don't have to be a **vegetarian** to enjoy the occasional meat- or fish-free meal, as these **delicious** dishes show. Here, you'll find recipes that make use of all kinds of **wonderful** ingredients from root **vegetables** and squashes to **beans** and pulses.

Many of the recipes in this chapter are based on vegetables that retain their shape and texture beautifully in the slow cooker. There are plenty of familiar favourites such as goulash and ratatouille and more unusual recipes from different cuisines that are destined to become your new favourites.

If you don't eat meat there are lots of other protein sources such as cheese, nuts and pulses. Do make sure that you get plenty of vitamins and minerals in your diet, including iron; as well as eggs, other non-meat sources of this vital mineral include dried fruit such as apricots, which you'll find in the Vegetable Curry (see page 226).

spiced bean & pumpkin stew

4

20 MINS

3 hrs AUTO

crusty wholemeal
(whole wheat)
bread

1 **large onion**, chopped

1 **garlic clove**, crushed

5 ml/1 tsp **sweet paprika**

2.5 ml/½ tsp dried **chilli flakes** or chilli purée (paste)

250 ml/8 fl oz/1 cup hot **vegetable stock**

700 g/1½ lb prepared **pumpkin** or **squash**, cut into 2.5 cm/1 in cubes

450 g/1 lb **sweet potatoes**, cut into 2.5 cm/1 in cubes

175 g/6 oz trimmed **okra (ladies' fingers)** or **French (green) beans**

1 x 400 g/14 oz/large **can of cannellini or haricot (navy) beans**, drained and rinsed

250 ml/8 fl oz/1 cup **passata (sieved tomatoes)**

Salt and freshly ground black pepper

1   Put the onion, garlic, paprika and chilli into the ceramic cooking pot. Pour over the stock, cover with the lid and switch on the slow cooker to Auto or Low. Leave for 3–4 minutes while preparing and measuring the remaining ingredients.

2   Add the pumpkin or squash and sweet potato cubes, the okra or French beans and the cannellini or haricot beans to the ceramic cooking pot. Pour over the passata and season with salt and pepper.

3   Stir everything together, then re-cover and cook for 3 hours or until the vegetables are very tender.

4   Serve straight away on a warmed plate, accompanied by crusty wholemeal bread.

Tip

• Passata is made from ripe tomatoes that have been puréed and sieved to remove the seeds and skins. It comes in jars and once opened can be kept in the refrigerator for up to a week or if you prefer, decant it into freezerproof containers and freeze for up to 2 months.

vegetable curry

| 4 | 30 MINS | 2-3 hrs HIGH | plain boiled rice, naan bread or chappatis |

V
Suitable for Vegetarians

1 **large onion**, chopped

2 **garlic cloves**, crushed or 10 ml/2 tsp garlic purée (paste)

10 ml/2 tsp freshly grated **root ginger** or ginger purée (paste)

30 ml/2 tbsp **medium curry powder**

2.5 ml/½ tsp **ground turmeric**

2 fresh **curry leaves**

900 ml/1½ pints/3¾ cups hot **vegetable stock**

225 g/8 oz **potatoes**, cut into 1 cm/½ in cubes

225 g/8 oz **aubergine (eggplant)**, cut into 1 cm/½ in cubes

1 **carrot**, cut into 1 cm/½ in cubes

175 g/6 oz fresh or frozen **green beans**

75 g/3 oz/½ cup **no-need-to-soak dried apricots**, chopped

30 ml/2 tbsp chopped **fresh or frozen coriander (cilantro)**

Salt and freshly ground black pepper

1 Put the onion, garlic, ginger, curry powder, turmeric and curry leaves into the ceramic cooking pot. Pour over the stock, cover with the lid and switch on the slow cooker to Low. Leave for 4–5 minutes while preparing and measuring the remaining ingredients.

2 Add the potato, aubergine, carrot, beans and apricots. Re-cover with the lid and cook on High for 2–3 hours or on Low for 4–6 hours or until all the vegetables are tender.

3 Remove the curry leaves. Stir in the coriander, then season to taste with salt and pepper.

4 Serve accompanied by rice or warmed naan bread or chappatis.

Tips

- Fresh curry leaves add a wonderful authentic aromatic flavour to this dish and can be frozen for future use. If you can't get any, add a couple of bay leaves instead.
- Try serving with some bought cucumber raita or simply with a spoonful or two of thick plain yoghurt.

mixed bean hot-pot

Chef's note

This easy one-pot dish of beans and vegetables makes a nourishing winter main course and needs no accompaniments. The combination of passata, red wine vinegar and sugar gives it a tasty sweet and sour flavour.

4

30 MINS

4-6 hrs LOW

complete meal in itself

10 ml/2 tsp **light soft brown sugar**

15 ml/1 tbsp **red wine vinegar**

15 ml/1 tbsp **Worcestershire sauce** or dark soy sauce

1 **garlic clove**, crushed or 5 ml/ 1 tsp garlic purée (paste)

600 ml/1 pint/2½ cups **passata (sieved tomatoes)**

1 bunch of **spring onions (scallions)**, trimmed and sliced

2 x 400 g/14 oz/large **cans of mixed pulses**, drained and rinsed

225 g/8 oz **green beans**, trimmed and halved

225 g/8 oz **mushrooms**, sliced

550 g/1¼ lb **potatoes**, roughly cut into 2 cm/¾ in chunks

5 ml/1 tsp **dried mixed herbs**

Salt and freshly ground black pepper

1 Put the sugar, vinegar, Worcestershire or soy sauce and garlic into the ceramic cooking pot. Add a little passata and stir until blended. Stir in the rest of the passata.

2 Add the spring onions, pulses, green beans, mushrooms, potatoes and herbs. Season with salt and pepper, then stir everything together.

3 Cover with the lid and cook on Low for 4–6 hours or until the vegetables are tender.

Tip

- Cans of mixed pulses usually contain chick peas (garbanzos), soya beans, black-eyed beans, pinto beans, red kidney beans and adzuki beans. If you prefer you can use cans of your favourite beans instead.

curried lentil casserole

4

20 MINS

4-6 hrs AUTO

naan bread and thick plain yoghurt

Chef's note

Here's an easy vegetarian dish that makes a satisfying main course all on its own. It's similar to the delicious spicy dhals from India but is packed with chunky potatoes, carrots and parsnips, giving it a wonderful texture.

700 g/1½ lb **new potatoes**, scrubbed (unpeeled)

15 ml/1 tbsp **sunflower oil**

1 **onion**, chopped

2 **garlic cloves**, crushed or 10 ml/2 tsp garlic purée (paste)

30 ml/2 tbsp **curry paste**

750 ml/1¼ pints/3 cups hot **vegetable stock**

4 **carrots**, thickly sliced

2 **parsnips**, thickly sliced

100 g/4 oz/⅔ cup **red lentils**

Salt and freshly ground black pepper

60 ml/4 tbsp chopped **fresh coriander (cilantro)**

1 Halve the potatoes or cut them into 2.5 cm/1 in chunks to make the pieces equally sized.

2 Heat the oil in a frying pan, add the onion and cook for 5 minutes. Add the garlic and cook for 2–3 minutes until softened. Stir in the curry paste and cook for 1 minute, stirring all the time.

3 Turn off the heat. Stir in a little of the stock, then transfer the mixture to the ceramic cooking pot. Add the potatoes, carrots, parsnip, lentils and the remaining stock, then season with salt and pepper.

4 Stir to combine, then cover with the lid and switch on the slow cooker to Auto or High and cook for 1 hour. Leave on Auto or reduce the temperature to Low and cook for 3–5 hours or until the vegetables and lentils are very tender.

5 Stir in the coriander, then taste and adjust the seasoning if necessary.

6 Serve drizzled with a little yoghurt and naan bread, if liked.

Tip
- Other vegetables such as butternut squash, swede (rutabaga) or celeriac (celery root) may be used in this dish.

puy lentil vegetable stew

4

20 MINS

6-8 hrs LOW

crumbled Feta or goats' cheese and soda bread

V

Suitable for Vegetarians

15 ml/1 tbsp **sunflower oil**

2 **red onions**, cut into thin wedges

2 **garlic cloves**, crushed or 10 ml/2 tsp garlic purée (paste)

1 **red chilli**, seeded and chopped

1 **acorn squash**, peeled, seeded and sliced

1 **fennel bulb**, trimmed and sliced

175 g/6 oz/1 cup **Puy lentils**, rinsed

750 ml/1¼ pints/3 cups hot **vegetable stock**

2.5 ml/½ tsp **dried mixed herbs**

Salt and freshly ground black pepper

1   Heat the oil in a frying pan, add the onions, garlic and chilli and cook gently for 5 minutes until beginning to soften. Transfer to the ceramic cooking pot and add all the remaining ingredients.

2   Stir well, then cover with the lid and cook on Low for 6–8 hours or until both the lentils and vegetables are tender and most of the stock has been absorbed.

3   Serve the casserole with crumbled Feta or goats' cheese (or with toasted flaked almonds). Soda bread also makes a good accompaniment.

Tip

• Choose a small acorn squash about 450 g/1 lb in weight before preparation. Alternatively, you can use a wedge of pumpkin or another variety of squash.

bean chilli with cornbread

4

30 MINS, plus soaking time

6-8 hrs AUTO + **1 hr HIGH**

a green vegetable

200 g/7 oz/1 cup **dried red kidney beans**

1 **vegetable stock (bouillon) cube**

1 **bay leaf**

15 ml/1 tbsp **olive oil**

1 **onion**, finely chopped

2 **garlic cloves**, crushed or 10 ml/2 tsp garlic purée (paste)

2 **celery sticks**, sliced

5 ml/1 tsp **ground chilli**

5 ml/1 tsp **ground cumin**

2.5 ml/½ tsp **dried mixed herbs**

1 x 400 g/14 oz/large **can of chopped tomatoes**

10 ml/2 tsp **sun-dried tomato purée**

Salt and freshly ground black pepper

For the cornbread topping:

175 g/6 oz/1½ cups **cornmeal**

15 ml/1 tbsp **wholemeal (whole wheat)** or **plain (all-purpose) flour**

5 ml/1 tsp **baking powder**

A pinch of **salt**

1 **egg**, lightly beaten

175 ml/6 fl oz/¾ cup **milk**

1. Put the kidney beans in a bowl, cover with cold water and soak for at least 6 hours. Drain and rinse, then put in a saucepan with 750 ml/1¼ pints/3 cups of cold water. Bring to the boil, then boil rapidly uncovered for 10 minutes. Turn off the heat, crumble in the stock cube and stir to dissolve. Leave to cool.

2. Tip the beans and their liquid into the ceramic cooking pot. Add the bay leaf. Cover and switch on to Auto or High.

3. Heat the oil in a frying pan, add the onion and cook for 3 minutes. Add the garlic and celery and cook for 3 more minutes. Stir in the chilli, cumin and herbs and cook for a few seconds, then add the mixture to the pot.

4. Cover and cook for 1 hour, then reduce to Low and cook for a further 5–7 hours or until the beans are very tender.

5. Remove the bay leaf. Stir in the tomatoes, tomato purée and salt and pepper. Increase to High and cook for 15 minutes.

6. Meanwhile, to make the topping, put the cornmeal, flour, baking powder and a pinch of salt in a bowl and stir together. Make a well in the middle, add the egg and milk and mix to a stiff batter. Spoon over the bean mixture and cook for a further 45 minutes or until the topping is well risen and firm.

7. Serve with a green vegetable.

Tip
- Raw kidney beans contain toxins that are destroyed by the rapid boiling for 10 minutes in Step 1, so don't miss out this step.

mixed mushroom casserole

4

30 MINS

2-3 hrs HIGH +
1-2 hrs LOW

mashed potatoes and crusty French or garlic bread

15 g/½ oz/4 tbsp **dried porcini mushrooms**

350 g/12 oz **small button (pearl) onions**, unpeeled

15 ml/1 tbsp **olive oil**

1 **garlic clove**, crushed or 5 ml/1 tsp garlic purée (paste)

10 ml/2 tsp **plain (all-purpose) flour**

100 ml/3½ fl oz/scant ½ cup **white wine**

15 ml/1 tbsp **mushroom ketchup** or dark soy sauce

10 ml/2 tsp **cider vinegar** or **white wine vinegar**

1 **bay leaf**

1 sprig of **fresh thyme**

350 ml/12 fl oz/1⅓ cups **vegetable stock**

225 g/8 oz **small button mushrooms**

225 g/8 oz **oyster mushrooms**, sliced

100 g/4 oz **shiitake mushrooms**, sliced

Salt and freshly ground black pepper

30 ml/2 tbsp chopped **fresh parsley**

1 Put the porcini mushrooms in a small heatproof bowl and pour over boiling water. Leave for about 15 minutes. Put the onions in another heatproof bowl and pour over enough boiling water to cover. Leave for 5 minutes.

2 Drain the onions and peel off the skins when cool enough to handle. Heat the oil in a frying pan and cook the onions until golden, turning frequently. Stir in the garlic and flour and cook for a further minute.

3 Add the wine, a little at a time and bring to the boil, stirring until thickened. Turn off the heat and stir in the mushroom ketchup or soy sauce and vinegar. Leave to cool for a minute.

4 Put the bay leaf and thyme in the ceramic cooking pot, then pour in the onions and wine mixture. Stir in the stock, then cover with the lid and cook on High for 2–3 hours or until the onions are almost tender.

5 Drain any excess water from the porcini mushrooms, add them to the pot with the other mushrooms and season with a little salt and pepper. Re-cover and reduce the temperature to Low. Cook for a further 1–2 hours or until the mushrooms and onions are tender. Remove the bay leaf and thyme sprig. Serve on warmed serving plates and sprinkle with the chopped parsley.

6 Serve with mashed potatoes and crusty French or garlic bread.

Tip

• If liked, the sauce can be reduced by tipping the mushroom casserole into a colander over a saucepan (return the mushrooms and onions and a few spoonfuls of liquid to the slow cooker and keep warm on a Low setting). Briskly boil the liquid for about 5 minutes, until slightly reduced. Pour back over the mushroom mixture.

egg-topped ratatouille

4 **25 MINS** **4-5 hrs AUTO + 15 mins HIGH** freshly shaved Parmesan cheese and warm crusty bread

450 g/1 lb **ripe plum tomatoes**, chopped or 1 x 400 g/14 oz/large **can of chopped tomatoes**

150 ml/¼ pint/⅔ cup hot **vegetable stock**

30 ml/2 tbsp **olive oil**

2 **red onions**, chopped

2 **garlic cloves**, crushed or 10 ml/2 tsp garlic purée (paste)

1 large **aubergine (eggplant)**, trimmed and cut into 1 cm/½ in dice

1 **yellow (bell) pepper**, seeded and sliced

1 **red pepper**, seeded and sliced

2 **courgettes (zucchini)**, trimmed and sliced

Salt and freshly ground black pepper

4 **eggs**

60 ml/4 tbsp torn **fresh basil leaves**

1 Put the tomatoes and stock in the ceramic cooking pot, cover with the lid and switch on the slow cooker to High or Auto.

2 Heat the oil in a frying pan, add the onion and cook for 5–6 minutes until fairly soft. Add the garlic and cook for 1 minute. Add to the cooking pot with all the remaining vegetables.

3 Season with salt and pepper, mix well, then re-cover and cook for 1 hour. Leave on Auto or turn down the temperature to Low and cook for a further 3–4 hours or until the vegetables are tender. If possible, stir the mixture halfway through the cooking time.

4 Stir the ratatouille mixture and turn up the temperature to High. Make four small hollows. Break the eggs, one at a time on to a saucer, then gently tip one in each hollow. Re-cover and cook for a further 15 minutes or until the egg white is set and the yolk is still soft, or a little longer if you prefer the egg firmer.

5 Carefully spoon the ratatouille mixture and the eggs on to warmed serving plates.

6 Scatter with the basil and Parmesan shavings and serve at once with warm crusty bread.

Tip

• Some vegetables cook more quickly than others in the slow cooker and the courgette will be very soft by the end of the cooking time. If you prefer a firmer texture, add it to the cooking pot 2 hours after the other vegetables.

vegetable crumble

Chef's note

Crumbles don't have to be sweet. This colourful, one-pot version with its oat, nut and cheese topping is ideal for a midweek meal and needs no accompaniment. Sweet potatoes are readily available in major supermarkets as well as ethnic food stores.

4

25 MINS

5-6 hrs LOW

complete meal in itself

25 g/1 oz/2 tbsp **butter**

2 **leeks**, thinly sliced

100 g/4 oz **button mushrooms**

1 **carrot**, cut into chunks

450 g/1 lb **sweet potatoes**, cut into chunks

5 ml/1 tsp **plain (all-purpose) flour**

100 g/4 oz **cream cheese** or **Mascarpone cheese**

250 ml/8 fl oz/1 cup **vegetable stock**

Salt and freshly ground black pepper

For the crumble topping:

100 g/4 oz/1 cup **plain (all-purpose) flour**

50 g/2 oz/¼ cup **butter**

50 g/2 oz/½ cup **grated Cheddar cheese**

30 ml/2 tbsp **rolled oats**

1   Melt the butter in a frying pan, add the leeks and mushrooms and cook gently for 5 minutes or until almost tender. Stir in the carrot and sweet potato.

2   Sprinkle the flour over the vegetables and stir in, then add the cream or Mascarpone cheese. Gradually stir in the stock. Continue stirring over a low heat until the mixture is bubbling and thickened. Season to taste with salt and pepper.

3   Leave to cool for 1 minute, then transfer the vegetable mixture to the ceramic cooking pot. Cover with the lid, switch on the slow cooker to Low and cook for 4–5 hours.

4   To make the crumble topping, sift the flour into a bowl and rub in the butter until the mixture resembles fine breadcrumbs. Stir in the cheese and oats.

5   Sprinkle the topping over the vegetables, re-cover and cook for a further hour. If your ceramic cooking pot can be used under the grill (broiler) – check the instruction booklet for this information – brown the top under a moderate grill before serving.

Tip
- If you prefer, leave out Step 5 and spoon the cooked vegetable mixture into an ovenproof gratin dish, sprinkle over the topping and bake at 190°C/375°F/gas 5/fan oven 170°C for 30 minutes.

vegetable goulash

4   **30 MINS**   **6-8 hrs AUTO**   thick plain or Greek yoghurt

15 ml/1 tbsp **olive oil**

1 **onion**, chopped

2 **garlic cloves**, crushed or 10 ml/2 tsp garlic purée (paste)

15 ml/1 tbsp **ground paprika**

350 g/12 oz **small new potatoes**, scrubbed (unpeeled)

1 **small cauliflower**, cut into small florets

4 **carrots**, thickly sliced

1 **butternut squash**, peeled, seeded and diced

1 x 400 g/14 oz/1 large **can of chick peas (garbanzos)**, drained and rinsed

600 ml/1 pint/2½ cups **tomato juice**

5 ml/1 tsp **dried mixed herbs**

Salt and freshly ground black pepper

1   Heat the oil in a frying pan, add the onion and cook for 7–8 minutes or until soft. Stir in the garlic, then sprinkle the paprika over and cook for a few more seconds.

2   Transfer the mixture to the ceramic cooking pot and switch on the slow cooker to Auto or High. Add all the remaining ingredients and stir well.

3   Cover with the lid and cook for 1 hour. Leave the slow cooker on Auto or reduce the temperature to Low and cook for a further 5–7 hours until the vegetables are tender.

4   Spoon the goulash on to warmed plates and serve topped with thick plain or Greek yoghurt.

spiced vegetables

| 4 | 25 MINS | 3-5 hrs HIGH | rice |

30 ml/2 tbsp **sunflower oil**

1 **onion**, sliced

2 **garlic cloves**, crushed or 10 ml/2 tsp garlic purée (paste)

1 **red chilli**, seeded and finely sliced

2.5 cm/1 in piece of **fresh root ginger**, grated or 10 ml/2 tsp **bottled grated ginger**

5 ml/1 tsp **ground turmeric**

5 ml/1 tsp **ground coriander**

2.5 ml/½ tsp **ground cumin**

1 **small cauliflower**, broken into small florets

1 **large sweet potato**, diced

2 **carrots**, sliced

150 ml/¼ pint/⅔ cup hot **vegetable stock**

45 ml/3 tbsp **ground almonds**

250 ml/8 fl oz/1 cup **coconut milk**

Salt and freshly ground black pepper

45 ml/3 tbsp chopped **fresh coriander (cilantro)**

45 ml/3 tbsp **toasted flaked (slivered) almonds**

1   Heat the oil in a large frying pan and cook the onion for 5–6 minutes, until beginning to soften. Stir in the garlic, chilli, ginger, turmeric, ground coriander and cumin and cook for 1 minute, stirring all the time.

2   Add the cauliflower, sweet potato, carrots and a few spoonfuls of the stock and stir to coat in the mixture. Tip into the ceramic cooking pot.

3   Add the ground almonds to the frying pan with the rest of the stock and bring to the boil, stirring. Turn off the heat and stir in the coconut milk.

4   Season with salt and pepper and pour the mixture over the vegetables. Cover with the lid and cook on High for 3–5 hours or on Low for 5–8 hours, or until the vegetables are tender.

5   Taste and adjust the seasoning if necessary, then stir in the chopped coriander.

6   Serve on a bed of rice, scattered with toasted flaked almonds.

Tip

• This recipe doesn't use a whole can of coconut milk, so if preferred use block creamed coconut (which will keep for a month in the refrigerator) and prepare the amount needed, following the packet instructions.

moroccan hot-pot

4 | **25** MINS | **5-7** hrs LOW | couscous and harissa sauce

Chef's note

Based on a tagine, this dish can be given authentic Middle Eastern flavours by serving it on a bed of steamed couscous and drizzling with harissa sauce.

V

Suitable for Vegetarians

30 ml/2 tbsp **olive oil**

1 **onion**, chopped

2 **garlic cloves**, crushed or 10 ml/2 tsp garlic purée (paste)

1 **red chilli**, seeded and finely sliced

5 ml/1 tsp **allspice**

1.5 ml/¼ tsp **saffron strands** or ground turmeric

2 **courgettes (zucchini)**, trimmed and cut into 2.5 cm/1 in chunks

1 **aubergine (eggplant)**, trimmed and cut into 2.5 cm/1 in chunks

2 **potatoes**, cut into 2.5 cm/1 in chunks

2 **carrots**, cut into 2.5 cm/1 in chunks

1 **cinnamon stick**

1 x 400 g/14 oz/large **can of chick peas (garbanzos)**, drained and rinsed

50 g/2 oz/⅓ cup **raisins**

50 g/2 oz/⅓ cup **no-need-to-soak dried apricots**

50 g/2 oz/⅓ cup stoned (pitted) **prunes**

Salt and freshly ground black pepper

750 ml/1¼ pints/3 cups **vegetable stock**

1 x 400 g/14 oz/large **can of chopped tomatoes**

45 ml/3 tbsp chopped **fresh coriander (cilantro)**

1   Heat the oil in a large frying pan and cook the onion for 5–6 minutes until beginning to soften. Stir in the garlic, chilli, allspice, saffron or turmeric and cook for a minute, stirring all the time. Transfer to the ceramic cooking pot.

2   Add the courgettes, aubergine, potatoes and carrots to the slow cooker with the cinnamon stick, chick peas, raisins, apricots and prunes. Season with salt and pepper.

3   Pour over the stock and chopped tomatoes. Gently stir everything together, then cover with the lid and cook on Low for 5–7 hours or until the vegetables are very tender.

4   Taste and adjust the seasoning if necessary, then stir in the chopped coriander.

5   Serve on a bed of couscous and drizzle with a little harissa sauce.

Tip
• Frying the spices before cooking in the slow cooker intensifies their flavour, so don't miss out this important step.

vegetable chilli

4

35 MINS

5-7 hrs LOW

rice or tacos

Chef's note

This is a great meatless chilli dish and if you have a large slow cooker it's worth making double the quantity and saving half for another day (it will keep in the refrigerator for 3 days or can be frozen). In addition to the serving suggestion below, it can be spooned on top of jacket potatoes.

V

Suitable for Vegetarians

15 ml/1 tbsp **sunflower oil**

1 **onion**, chopped

1 **garlic clove**, crushed or 5 ml/1 tsp garlic purée (paste)

1 **green chilli**, seeded and chopped

5 ml/1 tsp **mild chilli powder**

5 ml/1 tsp **ground cumin**

5 ml/1 tsp **ground paprika**

2.5 ml/½ tsp **dried oregano**

15 ml/1 tbsp **sun-dried tomato purée (paste)**

5 ml/1 tsp **light brown sugar**

5 ml/1 tsp **balsamic vinegar**

150 ml/¼ pint/⅔ cup hot **vegetable stock**

100 g/4 oz **button mushrooms**, sliced

1 **red (bell) pepper**, seeded and chopped

450 g/1 lb **mixed vegetables**, such as carrots, parsnips, potatoes, celery and aubergine (eggplant), cut into 1 cm/½ in dice

1 x 400 g/14 oz/large **can of chopped tomatoes**

1 x 400 g/14 oz/large **can of red kidney beans**, drained and rinsed

1 **bay leaf**

Salt and freshly ground black pepper

1   Heat the oil in a large frying pan. Add the onion and fry for 5–6 minutes or until beginning to soften.

2   Add the garlic, fresh chilli, chilli powder, cumin, paprika and oregano. Cook for 1 minute, stirring, then turn off the heat.

3   Stir the tomato purée, sugar and balsamic vinegar into the stock. Pour over the onion mixture and stir well, then tip into the ceramic cooking pot.

4   Add the mushrooms, chopped pepper, mixed vegetables, tomatoes, kidney beans, bay leaf, salt and pepper. Stir well.

5   Cover with the lid and cook on Low for 5–7 hours or until all the vegetables are tender and the chilli mixture is thick. Remove the bay leaf.

6   Serve with rice or tacos.

Tip

• To make filled tacos, warm the tacos in the oven according to the packet instructions, then spoon in the chilli. Top with shredded lettuce, soured (dairy sour) cream and chopped avocados and/or grated cheese.

meat-free bolognese

4

20 MINS

3-5 hrs LOW

spaghetti and grated Parmesan cheese

1 **onion**, chopped

1 **garlic clove**, crushed or 5 ml/ 1 tsp garlic purée (paste)

250 ml/8 fl oz/1 cup hot **vegetable stock**

450 g/1 lb **frozen soya mince** or **'meat-free' mince (ground soy)**, thawed

2 **carrots**, finely chopped

4 **mushrooms**, sliced

1 x 400 g/14 oz/large **can of chopped tomatoes**

10 ml/2 tsp **sun-dried tomato purée (paste)**

250 ml/8 fl oz/1 cup **red or white wine** or **extra vegetable stock**

5 ml/1 tsp **dried mixed herbs**

Salt and freshly ground black pepper

1 Put the onion and garlic in the ceramic cooking pot and pour over the stock. Cover with a lid and switch on the slow cooker to Low. Leave to cook for a few minutes while preparing and measuring the remaining ingredients.

2 Add the mince, carrots, mushrooms, chopped tomatoes, tomato purée, wine or extra stock and herbs to the cooking pot. Season with salt and pepper.

3 Stir well, then re-cover and cook for 3–5 hours or until the vegetables are very tender.

4 Serve spooned on top of cooked spaghetti. Sprinkle with some freshly grated Parmesan cheese, if liked.

Tip

• Turn this into a simple chilli by adding 1 x 400 g/14 oz/large can of red kidney beans, drained and rinsed, 10 ml/2 tsp mild chilli powder and 2.5 ml/½ tsp ground cumin in Step 2.

sweet & sour quorn casserole

4 | **15** MINS | **3-5** hrs AUTO | egg noodles or rice

V
Suitable for Vegetarians

15 ml/1 tbsp **cornflour (cornstarch)**

30 ml/2 tbsp **dark soy sauce**

15 ml/1 tbsp **balsamic vinegar**

15 ml/1 tbsp **hoisin sauce**

15 ml/1 tbsp **clear honey**

1 x 400 g/14 oz/large **can of pineapple pieces in natural juice**

120 ml/4 fl oz/½ cup hot **chicken stock**

400 g/14 oz packet of **chicken-style Quorn pieces**, thawed if frozen

500 g/18 oz packet of **frozen 'Chinese wok' vegetables**

Freshly ground black pepper

1   Put the cornflour in the ceramic cooking pot and add the soy sauce and balsamic vinegar. Stir together until blended, then stir in the hoisin sauce and honey.

2   Stir in the pineapple pieces and juice and the stock, then add the Quorn and vegetables. Season with a little pepper.

3   Cover with the lid and switch the slow cooker on to High or Auto. Cook for 1 hour, then switch to Low or leave on Auto and cook for a further 2–4 hours or until the vegetables are tender.

4   Serve with egg noodles or rice.

Tips
- Quorn pieces are made with mycoprotein, a member of the fungi family. Because it contains egg white, it is unsuitable for vegans.
- Frozen 'Chinese wok' vegetables are a mixture of beansprouts, carrots, sugar snap peas, water chestnuts, Chinese mushrooms, (bell) pepper, mustard green stems and ginger.

index